THE ART OF
Woodburning

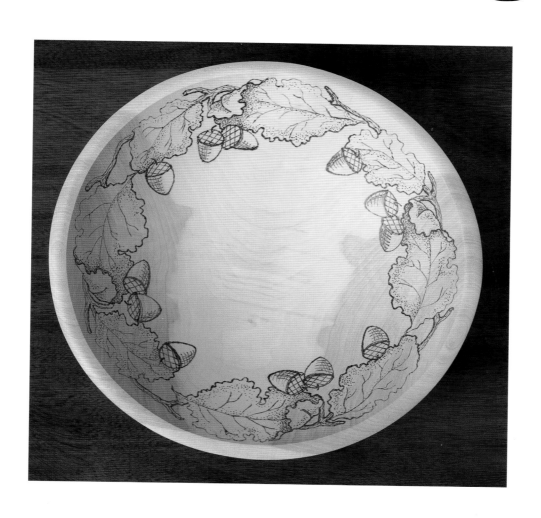

THE ART OF
Woodburning

30 Useful & Decorative Projects

Betty Auth

Sterling Publishing Co., Inc.
New York

Prolific Impressions Production Staff:

Editor: Mickey Baskett
Copy: Phyllis Mueller
Graphics: Dianne Miller, Karen Turpin
Styling: Lenos Key
Photography: Jerry Mucklow, Betty Auth
Administration: Jim Baskett

Library of Congress Cataloging-in-Publication Data Available

10 9 8 7 6 5 4

Published by Sterling Publishing Co., Inc.
387 Park Avenue South, New York, N.Y. 10016
Produced by Prolific Impressions, Inc.
160 South Candler St., Decatur, GA 30030
©2001, Prolific Impressions, Inc.
Distributed in Canada by Sterling Publishing
c/o Canadian Manda Group, 165 Dufferin Street
Toronto, Ontario, Canada M6K 3H6
Distributed in Great Britain by Chrysalis Books Group PLC
The Chrysalis Building, Bramley Road, London W10 6SP, England
Distributed in Australia by Capricorn Link (Australia) Pty. Ltd.
P.O. Box 704, Windsor, NSW 2756 Australia

For information about custom editions, special sales, premium and corporate purchases, please contact Sterling Special Sales Department at 800-805-5489 or specialsales@sterlingpub.com

About Betty Auth

Betty Auth is a designer, author, editor and artist. Her creativity spans many mediums, including woodburning, beading and wire work, needle arts such as crazy quilting and applique, cloth doll-making, scrap-booking and more. This is her second book on woodburning, following *Woodburning: 20 Great-Looking Projects To Decorate In A Weekend* (Lark Books, 1999).

Betty has published over 200 projects in national magazines such as *Better Homes and Gardens* publications, *Crafts Magazine, Craftworks, Arts and Crafts Magazine, The Cloth Doll* and others. She wrote a regular column for *Arts & Crafts* Magazine titled, "Ready, Set, Go!" Betty was the Crafts & Hobbies Editor for CraftShop.com, learning lots of valuable online techniques.

Betty has appeared on The Carol Duvall Show, her work was featured on HGTV's Home Matters, and she is a featured artisan in the Fall of 2000 on Lynette Jennings Designs. All of these appearances highlight the art and ease of woodburning.

Betty's recent honors in the *Society of Craft Designers* include: Finalist, Designer of the Year 1999; Designer With Heart 1999; member of the Board of Directors 1998-1999; Educational Seminar Co-Chair,1999; and chair of the Website Task Force 2000-2001.

Betty believes creativity belongs to everyone, and the most important gift we can give ourselves is the freedom to try something new without the limiting fear of failure. She practices what she preaches and will try almost any creative medium. Betty lives in Houston, Texas.

Acknowledgements:

The author would like to thank the following companies for their generosity in supplying product to use for creating the woodburned designs:

for woodburning tools, wood surfaces, and oil pencils:
Walnut Hollow
1409 State Red. 23
Dodgeville, WI 53533
www.walnuthollow.com

for Decorator Products clear and colored glazes:
Plaid Enterprises, Inc.
3225 Westech Dr.
Norcross, GA 30092
www.plaidonline.com

Table of Contents

Introduction
PAGE 9

History of Pyrography
PAGE 10

Supplies
Information on tools, equipment, surfaces, and coloring and staining supplies

PAGE 13

Woodburning Techniques
Preparing the woodburner, changing and cleaning points, burning wood, woodburning patterns

PAGE 20

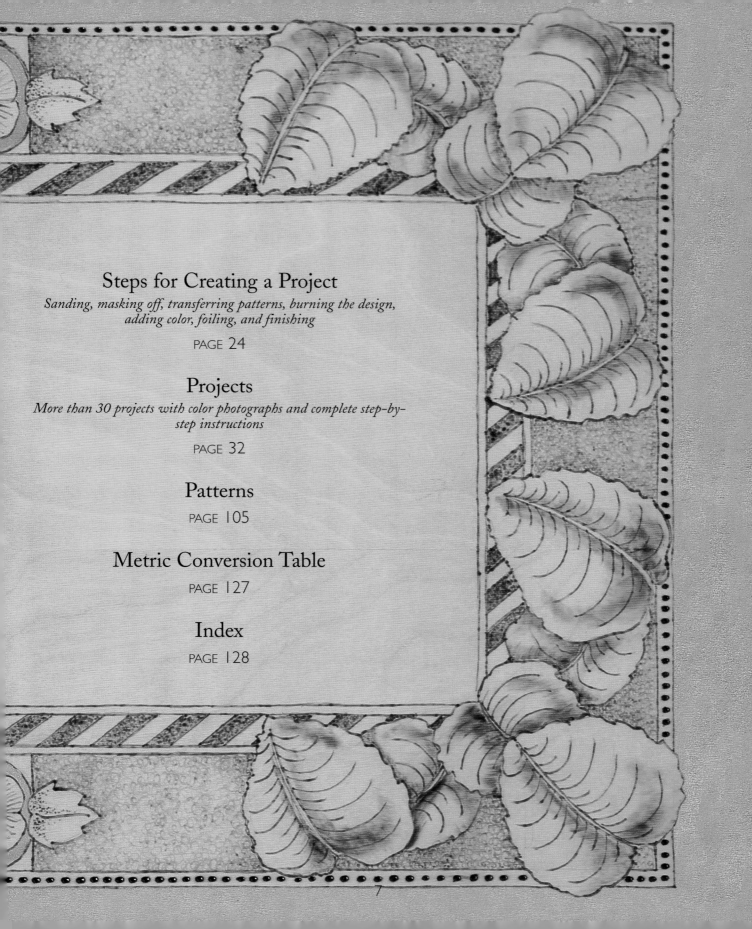

Learn an old-fashioned art that has a modern, rustic appeal.

Woodburning is a time-honored art and craft of burning designs into a wood surface. With a simple heating tool that has a sharp point, any design can be engraved into the wood—almost as easily as using a pencil on paper.

Woodburning a design results in a warm, rustic look that is so popular in today's decorating. A natural wood surface adorned with pinecones, ivy, or vining flowers results in a look that is popular in today's decorating—simple, natural and straight-forward. The plain wood surface, when impressed with graphic charm becomes not only a hard-working home decor accessory but a piece of art as well. A wooden salad bowl etched with a graphic acorn design is as impressive filled with garden greens as it is perched on a pedestal.

A wooden salad bowl etched with a graphic acorn design is as impressive filled with garden greens as it is perched on a pedestal.

This book tells you everything you need to know about choosing and gathering supplies, selecting wooden surfaces, and getting started. It includes historical information about the craft of woodburning, which the Victorians called pyrography. You'll also learn how to use woodburning tools and add color to your designs.

More than 30 projects, complete with color photographs, lists of supplies needed, and step-by-step instructions are presented to interest and inspire you. There are fabulous designs—from simple to ornate, vintage to modern—for furniture and accessories, including tables, cabinets, boxes, albums, and tabletop and wall pieces—even jewelry! Many projects are especially suitable for beginners.

Enjoy this exploration of woodburning and create something wonderful for your home! ❏

History of Pyrography

Pyrography was a term used in Victorian times for the art of woodburning. History is most meaningful when it relates to your own personal life, so that's the way I will tell it to you. The Victorian art of pyrography became meaningful to me when my mother gave me a woodburned box that her mother, my Grammie, had made.

Grammie was Florence Dorsey Schlitz, and she was born in 1881. After high school, she went away to secretarial school in San Francisco, and that's when she made the cherry-covered box. Although my box isn't signed or dated, Grammie made it in 1906, and the stamped, ready-to-burn basswood box sold at that time, probably through a mail-order catalogue, for twenty-five cents. That notation appears in pencil on the bottom of the box. It's typical of the items that were manufactured by the thousands around the turn of the 20th century.

In the 1890s, pyrography received a boost when a platinum point and a new woodburning outfit were introduced, making the craft possible for women and teenage girls to manage. Previously, woodburning had been done by heating several irons, or pokers, in an open fire, then sitting near the fire to work so a new poker

Above: A cherry-covered woodburned box made by the author's grandmother, Florence Dorsey Schlitz. Family legend says it was done in 1906 while Florence was away at business school.

Left: Pages from a Thayer & Chandler 1905 catalog. This Chicago firm was a mail order source for art supplies and pyrography goods. The wood pieces could be purchased raw, stamped with a design ready to burn, or already decorated.

could be picked up when the one being used had lost its heat. This was immensely hot and tedious work, and the results were not always beautiful because the poker was heavy and cumbersome. Fine details were impossible for the average person to achieve, and the craft was hardly worth the effort. The newly introduced platinum point was much more delicate, and it retained heat for a longer period of time. The point was attached to a tool that looked much like our electric tools today, but it was heated by a system of tubes, bellows and benzine. It may sound complicated and difficult to us today, but to Victorian girls and ladies it was a miracle that enabled them to decorate all kinds of boxes, shelves, chairs, plaques and other pre-stamped wooden items for their homes and for gifts.

I wrote about the 1906 cherry box in a magazine article, and then in a book. When my

aunt saw it, she mentioned that she had another woodburned piece among her treasure trove of family heirlooms. Imagine my surprise and delight when she told me that the second woodburned piece, a frame, was made by Grammie's mother! This one is signed "Xmas 09, L.D.D.," the initials of Lucy Dale Dorsey, who was born in 1858. We believe that Grammie brought the pyrography set home with her when she finished school,

Continued on next page

Above: A woodburned frame decorated with grapes, made by the author's great-grandmother, Lucy Dale Dorsey. On the back of the frame there is an inscription, "Christmas, 1909." This was a stamped design, but Lucy gave it her own creative interpretation, with evident changes. Lucy was 16 in the photo shown in frame. She was 51 when she wood-burned the frame, and 96 at her death.

Left: A brilliantly colored vintage Australian vase from the author's collection. This is a typical turn-of-the-century design.

and a couple of years later her mother picked it up and tried it. Careful examination of the grape design on the frame reveals faint stamped outlines underneath the burning. Lucy apparently took a little artistic license with the design and left out some of the grapes, adding her personal touch as she went.

Over the years, the craft of woodburning has come and gone, then come again as so many crafts have done. After World War II (in the 1940s and 1950s), there was a resurgence of popularity when kits were developed for young people. Many a pre-teen received a woodburning set for Christmas, but the points were difficult to use, and kids often lost interest very quickly. This scenario was repeated in the 1970s. This time, the kits were widely distributed through scouting and other youth groups. The same problem with the difficult point occurred, and the craft disappeared from the general scene once more. Today, the points are much improved and interchangeable, so they're much easier for beginners to use.

We often think of Victorian pyrography as plain brown, but lithographs from a 1905 catalog show brilliant color being incorporated into the designs, very much like the vintage Australian vase, with a predominance of deep, luscious reds. (The two family pieces shown here have no added color, possibly because the artists had no confidence in their ability to paint the pieces after they were burned.) Most woodburned items we see in antiques stores today are varying shades of brown, due to fading over the years. Sometimes, a glimmer of color can still be seen on them, even though a century has passed. Today's coloring agents and other improved supplies offer a range of possibilities for creating delightful heirlooms to pass down through the next century. ❏

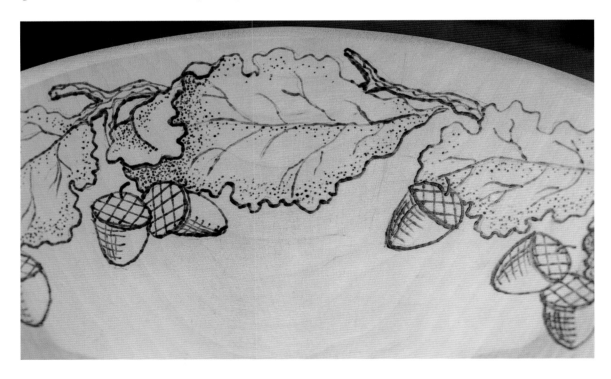

Supplies & Techniques

The "Supplies" section provides information on the tools, equipment, surfaces, and coloring and staining supplies you'll need to create your woodburning projects. You should be able to find these supplies in a craft or art supply shop, or at an internet source.

The "Techniques" section tells you everything you need to know to get started in this extraordinary woodburning craft. You will learn how to prepare the woodburner, change and clean points, and burn the wood. Examples of woodburning patterns are included.

The section on "Steps for Creating a Project" will lead you step-by-step through the stages of creating a project—such as sanding, masking off, transferring patterns, and burning the design. This chapter also illustrates some additional decorating techniques, including adding color, foiling, and finishing. ❑

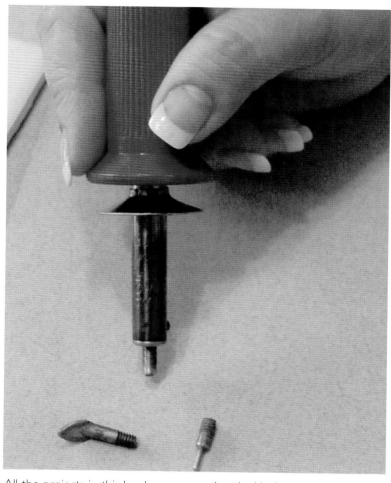

All the projects in this book were completed with three points: The Flow Point (shown in the burner) used for outlining and creating line designs; the Mini-Flow Point, a smaller version of the Flow Point used for linework and adding fine details; and the Shading Point (leaf-shaped) used for darkening large areas.

Woodburning Tool

All the projects in this book were completed using a solid shaft woodburning tool with interchangeable points. Three points were used for all these projects: the Flow Point, the Mini-flow Point, and the Shading Point. The solid shaft wood-burner is packaged with a wire holder and at least one woodburning point. A good starter point is the flow point, which has a rounded end and moves freely over the wood to produce a line.

Several point styles are available for specific purposes, and points can be purchased as an assortment that includes the most common ones. (The point most frequently supplied with the burner is called a universal point because it is intended as an all-purpose tool. However, it is probably the most difficult point to master and should be set aside until you become familiar with the other points.)

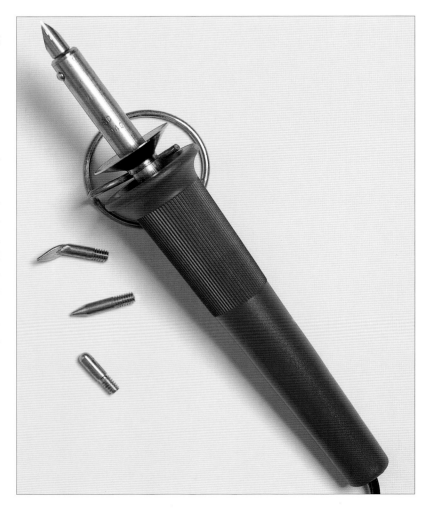

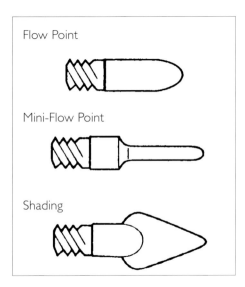

Flow Point

Mini-Flow Point

Shading

Once you have learned to use the three points I recommend, you may wish to experiment with some of the others or even try using a variable temperature-wire tip woodburning system. These systems are much more costly than the solid shaft tool and are designed for much more intricate detail work.

Cautions: Remember that the woodburning point will reach a temperature of 950 to over 1000 degrees Fahrenheit. It is perfectly safe to use as long as certain safety measures are taken, and the rules are followed. Children under 12 should not be allowed to use a woodburner without close adult supervision at all times, and a junior woodburning tool is recommended for them. It only reaches a temperature of between 600 to 750 degrees Fahrenheit.

Workspace Set-Up Supplies

In addition to the woodburning tool and the points, you'll need a few additional items when setting up your work space:

A **4" ceramic tile**, for taping down the wire holder for the woodburner. The tile is heavy enough so it won't move around on the work surface, and it is heatproof.

A **container**, such as a metal lid, a glass dish, or ceramic plate, to place the hot burner points in until they cool. When removed from the hot woodburner, the points retain their heat for a couple of minutes, so they need to be treated with care.

A pair of **needlenose pliers** with plastic or rubber-coated handles, for removing the hot point from the woodburner and replacing it with a different one. After changing a hot point, the pliers retain the heat for a couple of minutes, so it's a good idea to rest the metal part of the pliers on the points container until cool.

A folded **piece of sandpaper**, for cleaning carbon buildup from the hot point.

Aluminum foil or other heat-resistant material, to cover your work surface.

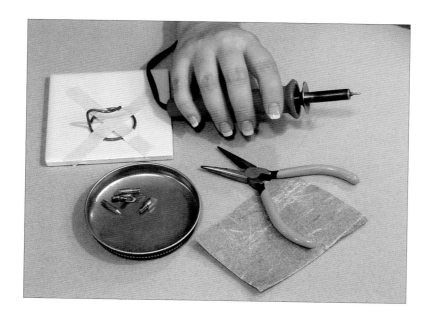

Wood Surfaces

The projects in this book are created with new, unfinished wooden furniture and accessories that are readily available at crafts and department stores and building supply centers. Many items are made of **basswood**, the favorite surface of most woodburning artists. Other popular woods for woodburning include **aspen, pine, poplar, red oak, and cedar**.

Old wooden furniture and accessories can be used for woodburning if all traces of varnish or other finishes are removed by thorough sanding.

If you like a particular pattern, but want to put it on a different piece of wood, take the pattern with you to the store to judge how it will look.

Varieties of Wood for Burning

The best woods for woodburning are light in color, even-grained, soft, and smooth. Almost any wood may be used except very thin plywood or veneer—they may contain adhesives that emit dangerous fumes when heated by the woodburning tool. Cabinet-grade plywood, which has at least a 1/4" thick ply, can be used. Following are favorite types of wood to use for woodburning:

Cedar can be very light, fairly smooth and medium hard when the inner core of the wood is used. Or, it can be rougher and darker, with a reddish cast if the bark is utilized. Cedar is a good wood for outdoor projects because it is impervious to moisture and resistant to changes in the weather. Cedar burns surprisingly well, although it may have some softer or harder spots, and contrast is not easily achieved because of the darkness of the wood. Mailboxes and birdhouses are often made of cedar, and can be woodburned to good effect. If you are sensitive to the fumes cedar may emit when heated, wear a face mask or direct a fan across the work while burning.

Basswood produces a very even, dark, consistent line much like **aspen** or **poplar**, but basswood burns darker.

Pine used for our example is cabinet grade, the very smoothest pine available. Much of the pine you find at crafts stores is of a lesser grade (and therefore is less expensive), but it produces dark and light spots when burned and may contain sap that will surface during burning, producing blotches and streaks. (This may be okay if your intent is a "folk art" or rustic appearance.)

Birch is a strong, lightly colored wood with a tight, smooth grain that burns slowly. Because of its hard surface, it burns lighter than some softer woods. To burn birch, use a large, rounded point.

Red Oak is beautiful wood, with surface graining that lends character. It has a rosy color and burns well because it is smooth and fine, but it can be somewhat hard. It is usually best for designs that have a lot of open areas because the graining of the wood may interfere with the clarity of more intricate woodburned patterns.

Examples of Wood for Woodburning

All five examples at right were decorated with the same pattern, using the same woodburning points. Outlines were done with a flow point, details were added with a mini-flow point, and the shadow at the base of each was completed with a shading point. The differences in appearance are the result of the different woods.

Pattern Transferring Materials

To transfer patterns, you'll need:
- **Tracing paper** and a **no. 2 lead pencil** for tracing the designs from the book.
- After enlarging the design on a photocopier, you'll need **scissors** to cut out the pattern to fit the surface, **masking tape** to tape the design in place, and **transfer paper** to slip under the design.
- Use a **pencil or ball point pen** to trace over the pattern lines, transferring the design to the wood. I prefer one with red lead or ink because it allows you to see where you have traced.
- You'll need an **eraser** to remove pattern lines after you've finished woodburning.

Supplies for Colored Pencil Work

The best pencils for coloring on wood are **oil color pencils**, which are constructed of an oil pigment contained in a wax base. The pencils come in a large array of colors and can be layered and blended. Because these pencils are made of wax, they are as comfortable and familiar as the crayons you probably used as a child.

The pencils need to be kept sharp, so you'll need an **electric or battery-operated pencil sharpener**. Sometimes, pencil artists hone the points with a razor-sharp knife to prevent waste, but unless you're coloring a very large surface, this isn't necessary.

Staining & Glazing Supplies

Neutral glazing medium is a transparent liquid or gel that can be mixed with **colored glazing gels** or high-quality **artist's acrylic paints** in true pigment colors to create transparent glazes and stains. These glazes can be used to add color to your woodburned designs. The medium's long drying time allows you to blot and rub colors for a variety of effects. An 8-oz. bottle or jar is enough for several projects.

Acrylic crafts paints, pre-mixed in a huge range of colors and glittering metallics, are used for trimming and accents. Artist's acrylics, acrylic craft paints, and glazing medium are available at crafts and art supply stores.

You'll need several **paintbrushes**: a large, flat soft bristle brush or sponge brush for applying varnish, a smaller flat brush for painting, glazing, and varnishing tight areas, and a small round brush for painting details.

Finishing Supplies

- **Spray-on matte acrylic sealer** is used for sealing the insides of boxes and sealing oil pencil coloring. Matte sealer spray can be used as a final sealer on pieces that won't get heavy use.
- **Brush-on acrylic varnish**, available in matte, satin, and gloss sheens, is used to finish pieces that get heavy use and as a sealer to mask areas of designs to protect them from stains or glazes.

General Supplies

- Sanding is important when woodburning. You'll need some **fine grit sandpaper** and, if desired, a block of wood to tape it around.
- Use **recycled plastic containers** with lids for mixing stains and glazes—you can mix more stain than you need immediately, then put on the lid and save it for up to a few days. The lids are also good for mixing colors. A **glass jar** can also be used for mixing.
- Recycled cotton athletic socks make terrific **rags** for blotting and rubbing down stains and glazes, as do old, soft terrycloth towels. Rags should be clean and free of lint.
- Use **masking tape** for securing the woodburner's wire holder to the tile, for holding the pattern to the wood surface while transferring designs, and for protecting areas from accidental burns.
- It's handy to have a half-and-half **ink/pencil eraser**. The smooth white plastic end is excellent for removing lead pencil or oil pencil from wood without damaging the surface. When you need more eraser power, the gray end of the eraser, which has a gritty substance imbedded in it, acts as an abrasive to remove those difficult marks. If you can't find a half-and-half eraser, choose a white plastic one and use very fine grit **sandpaper** for persistent marks.
- Use **cotton swabs** to move the oil pencil wax around on the surface to blend the colors and make them smooth.

WOODBURNING TECHNIQUES

Preparing the Woodburner

All the projects in this book were completed using a solid shaft woodburning tool with three interchangeable points. Remember that the point of the woodburning tool will reach a temperature of 950 to over 1000 degrees Fahrenheit. It is perfectly safe if used correctly.

To set up your woodburner, tape the wire holder that comes with it to a ceramic tile. Then tape the tile to the work surface to secure it. Use needlenose pliers to insert a point into the end of the woodburner shaft. Tighten to secure. Rest the woodburner on the wire holder and plug it in. It will take four or five minutes to heat fully. Whenever the burner is not in use, rest it on the wire holder. Unplug it when you finish the woodburning portion of your design.

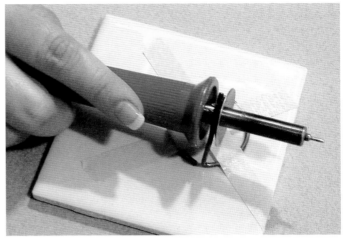
Preparing the woodburner

Changing Points

While the woodburner is hot, it is possible to change points by using rubber or plastic-handled needlenose pliers. **Never** touch any metal part of the woodburner with your fingers. **Always** use pliers. Firmly grasp the point with the tip of the pliers holding the plastic shaft of the woodburner in the other hand. Twist the point counter-clockwise, remove it, and immediately place the hot point in a glass, tin, or ceramic receptacle. The point will retain its heat for several minutes, and the receptacle will get hot. Pick up your chosen point with the pliers and insert it into the shaft, tightening securely.

Changing points

Cleaning the Point

While woodburning, you will probably accumulate ash, carbon, and other debris on the point. Keep a square of medium grit sandpaper handy. Occasionally wipe the point across the sandpaper to clean off the debris. Check the cooled points occasionally and sand them as needed to keep them bright and shiny.

Cleaning the point

Burning the Wood

The beauty of woodburning is accented by deep contrast and variety of pattern. To achieve the darkest, deepest burn, hold the woodburner as you would a pen or pencil, and move at about half the speed you would use when writing or drawing. While burning, keep the point moving. If you stop, lift the point from the surface of the wood to avoid dark blotches, spots, and unwanted burns. The darkness of the burn is controlled by the length of time the point is touching the wood, not by pushing the point into the wood.

Outlining: Most of the time, you will want to maintain a solid, even, flowing line that follows a pattern line. The best way to achieve this is to hold the burner lightly, turning the wood as you go so that you are pulling the line toward you rather than pushing it away from you. This will help avoid pushing too hard into the wood. For small skips in the line, re-burn the area with short "chicken scratching" or sketching movements.

Practice on a scrap of wood or the back of your wooden piece before starting any projects. You might practice by first penciling, then burning your name and the date.

If you accidentally make a small burning error, you may be able to sand it away with fine grit sandpaper, then erase remaining marks with an ink eraser. Larger errors are permanent, and you will need to find a way to incorporate them into your design.

Hold the burner like you would hold a brush or pencil, letting it rest naturally in your hand. Do not touch any of the metal parts. Practice by writing your name on the back of your chosen piece of wood. Write very slowly, letting the point flow across the surface of the wood. Lift the point from the surface when you begin or end a line to avoid making a darker dot.

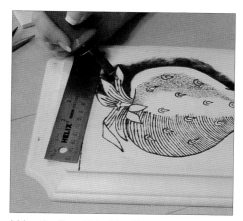

Using the Flow Point. The Flow Point is the most commonly used point for projects in this book. It is good for outlining designs and creating many of the line patterns as shown on the following page. The Flow Point is excellent for harder woods and for achieving a solid line on rougher pine surfaces.

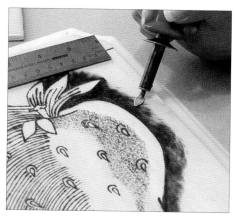

Using the Shading Point. The Shading Point is held with the leaf-shaped bottom of the point flat against the wood while the point is moved in small circles. It can also be dragged slowly along the outside edge of an object or design to create a shadow effect. Practice to discover the precise angle that produces the best deep, dark color for your own personal touch.

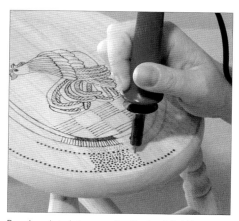

Burning dots into wood with the Mini-Flow Point. The Mini-Flow Point makes a line just a bit narrower than the Flow Point. It is good for adding the finer details in your design such as dots and stippling. To make even, round dots, the tool is held perpendicular to the surface and the point is touched to the wood, then lifted again. Holding the point to the surface longer will create larger dots. If you touch and lift very quickly, you will create a stippled look.

Woodburning Patterns

*After **Outlining** a pattern, you may wish to fill in areas with pattern. Here are some patterns that can be used. Descriptions are keyed to the numbers in the photograph and describe each oval example from top to bottom.*

1. **DOTS** can be used to create borders and backgrounds or designs. The ones on the upper part of the oval were made with a flow point—first scattered, then evenly spaced. The dots on the lower part were made with a mini-flow point—first scattered, then evenly spaced, then scattered again.

2. **FILL-IN PATTERNS,** are just what their name says—they fill in an area of a design. Here, the mini-flow point was used. On the top half, small circles are loosely formed, then densely burned. On the bottom half, back-and-forth lines are densely burned, then lightly burned.

3. **HATCHING** fills a space with groups of short parallel lines; cross hatching adds a second set of parallel lines angled at approximately 90 degrees from the first set. On the top half here, the mini-flow point was used to create medium dense cross hatching, then less dense hatching. On the lower half, the flow point was used to create hatching close together, then with larger lines farther apart.

4. **BASKET WEAVE PATTERNS** are regularly spaced lines that look like woven reeds. On the upper area, the flow point was used to create a smaller weave with wider lines. On the lower area, the mini-flow point was used for a larger weave with thinner lines.

5. **STIPPLING** uses tiny touches of the point to create patterns and shading. Here the mini-flow point was used to create scattered stippling that becomes closer together. Farther down, the flow point was used to gradually increase the density.

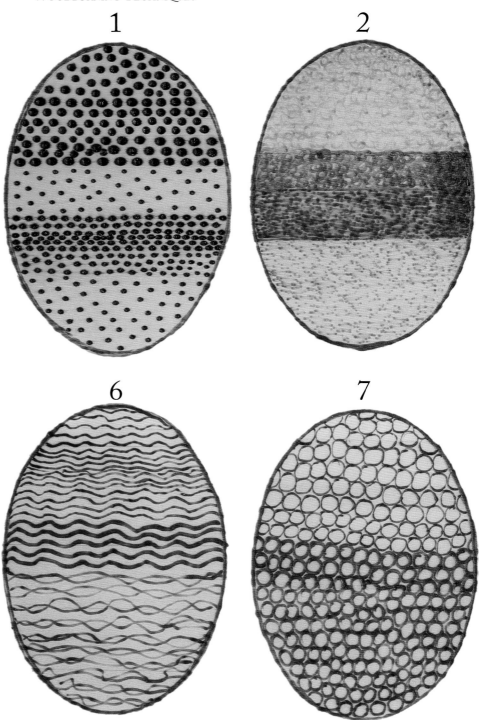

6. **WAVY LINES** can be parallel or overlapping. In the upper section, the mini-flow point was used to create even, parallel waves that increase in density. Near the center, the flow point created even waves, then uneven, crossed-over lines.

7. **CIRCLES** can be used to fill a space. Here, the mini-flow point created medium circles that touch. At the center, the flow point was used to make smaller circles burned very slowly, then less dark ones.

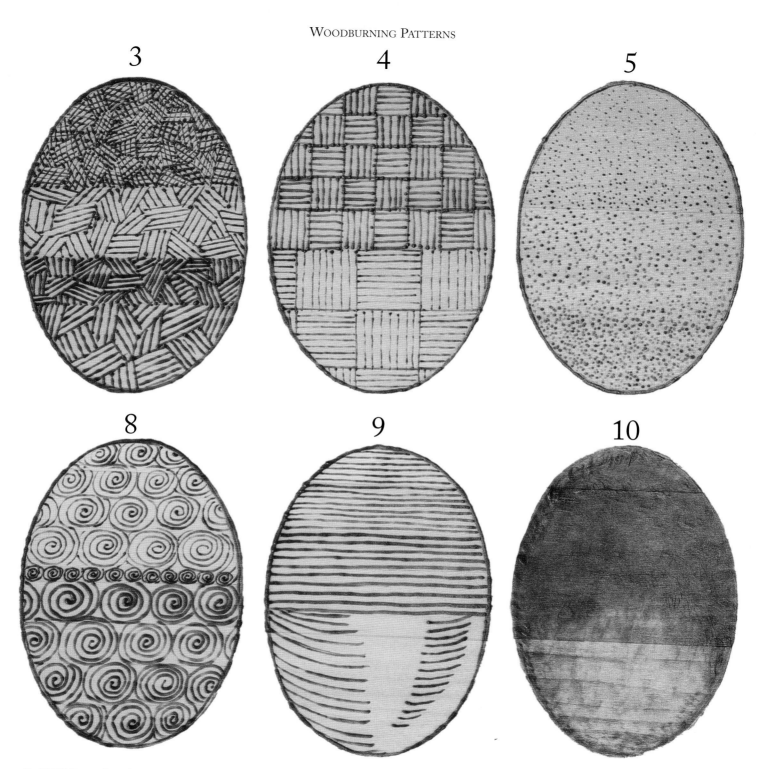

8. **COILS** can be of any size. At the top, the mini-flow point was used to make evenly spaced coils with thinner lines, then very small coils. On the lower half, the flow point was used to make evenly spaced coils.

9. **PARALLEL LINES** can fill space and indicate shapes. On the top third, the mini-flow point was used to make straight, evenly spaced lines. On the bottom half, the flow point was used to make thicker, straight lines, then curved lines that follow the shape of the object.

10. **SHADING** can be dense or light. Here, the shading point is used to create dark and dense shading that fades away toward the bottom of the oval. Drag the shading point slowly and evenly for dark shading; for light shading, move the point in a circular motion.

STEPS FOR CREATING A PROJECT

~ 1 ~
Sanding

All the projects in this book were created with new, unfinished wood pieces and furniture. Even if wood is new and appears clean, it still needs to be sanded to remove the oils that are transferred from hands and to smooth any rough spots or burrs created by the cutting process. Sanding also seems to open up the pores of the wood so the surface more readily accepts woodburning and the woodburning appears darker.

Remove any hardware before starting to work on the piece. Sand with the grain when possible and take care to sand inside curves and along outside edges. On inside curves, fold a small piece of medium sandpaper and smooth rough areas evenly. Replace the sandpaper from time to time as the grit wears off. On outside edges, tape a piece of medium sandpaper around a scrap of wood to make a sanding block or use a purchased sanding block. While sanding, you also may wish to round off the sharp edges on straight pieces of wood.

~ 2 ~
Masking Off Surfaces

If you are burning a design close to an edge or a lip that is not to be burned, it's a good idea to protect the area from accidental burns. To do this, cover areas you want to protect with two layers of masking tape. This needs to be done only to areas that are near any areas that will be woodburned.

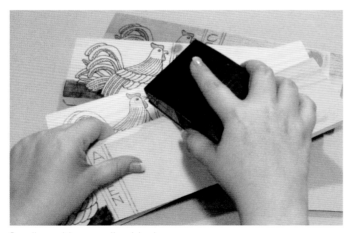
Sanding with a sanding block.

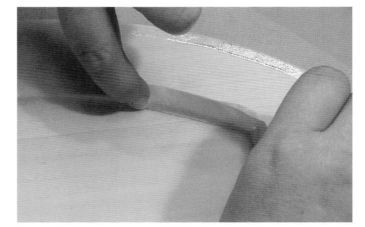
Applying masking tape.

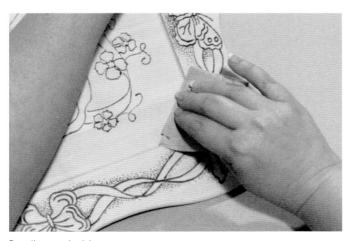
Sanding an inside curve.

Burning next to a taped area.

Transferring a cutout pattern.

≈ 3 ≈
Transferring the Pattern

Because of their large size, many of the patterns for these projects must be enlarged before tracing and transferring them to the wood. To use the patterns in this book, trace them onto tracing paper using a ballpoint pen. Then enlarge them to fit your project using a photocopier. You can also enlarge them by hand using graph paper. After enlarging, cut out pieces of the pattern and tape them to the surface where you want to place the design. This allows you to see the design placement as you transfer it. Cut graphite paper into 3" or 4" squares and slip a piece under the pattern. Use a red pencil or ballpoint pen to go over the pattern lines to transfer them. (Red makes it easier to see what part of the design you've already traced.) Move the graphite paper around as you transfer the design.

≈ 4 ≈
Burning the Design

Use the woodburner with the specified point to trace over the pattern lines for outlining and to create shading on the wood surface. See the "Techniques" section for information on holding and handling the woodburner and the patterns and effects that can be created.

After the woodburning is completed, go over the entire wood surface with an eraser to eliminate any traces of pencil or graphite that may remain after transferring and burning. Even if they cannot be seen, these tiny bits can cause your coloring agent to lose its clarity and become gray or dirty.

Instructions for "Two Fishes Box" are on page 69

∼ 5 ∼
Coloring the Design

There are three options for adding color to your project **after** the woodburning is complete:

- Staining
- Painting & Glazing
- Coloring with Oil Pencils

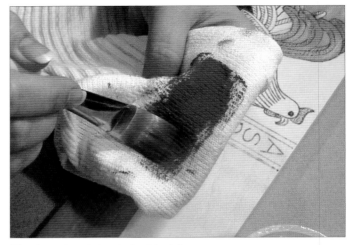
Blotting a brush loaded with stain on a rag.

Staining Techniques

Staining is the application of transparent wood-toned pre-mixed wood stains, antiquing mediums, or mixes of brown-tone paint and glazing medium to large or small areas of an entire project or to highlight or shade a part of a design. Two staining methods are used in this book—the first is rubbing on the stain, the second is painting, then blotting the stain. With either method, some stain may be removed after application with a slightly damp clean rag.

PAINTING, THEN BLOTTING

Dip a brush in stain and blot the brush on a rag. Brush the stain directly on the wood in the direction of the grain. Wipe off some of the stain with a clean rag as you go.

Applying stain with a brush.

RUBBING ON THE STAIN

For small areas, wrap a clean portion of a rag around your finger, dip it lightly into the stain, and rub it on the wood. Turn to a clean area of the rag and rub off as much stain as desired, taking care to always rub **away** from any design elements. On larger areas, apply some stain on the rag with a brush, scrunch the rag up in your hand, and rub the stain on the wood, again avoiding the design elements.

Applying stain with a rag.

26

Painting & Glazing

Artist's acrylics or craft paints can be used to highlight a design or mixed with a neutral glazing medium to create a richly pigmented, semi-transparent glaze that can be wiped off to reveal the woodburning underneath. The glazing process is very simple and can be adjusted to achieve the depth of color you want. **Always** mix enough glaze to finish your project—it can be difficult to match the color density if you run out. Finish glazing with one color before applying a second. Here are the steps:

1. Pour about two tablespoons of glazing medium in a plastic container. Add 1 teaspoon acrylic paint. (Amounts may differ based on the project—individual project instructions include suggested amounts.) Mix well.
   For the remaining steps, work on one small area at a time so the glaze will not soak into the wood before you have a chance to finish the process.

2. Brush a generous amount of glaze on the wood, covering the design and the woodburning. Try to stay within the design lines.

3. Blot excess glaze with a clean, soft rag to avoid smears and overruns. Lay the rag directly on the glaze and gently press for a few seconds. Lift the rag from the surface without moving it from side to side. If excess glaze remains, repeat.

Continued on next page

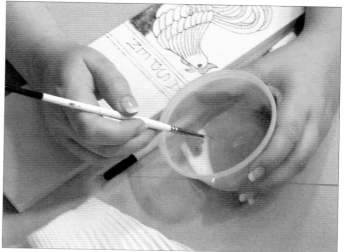
Mixing the glaze.

Applying the glaze with a brush.

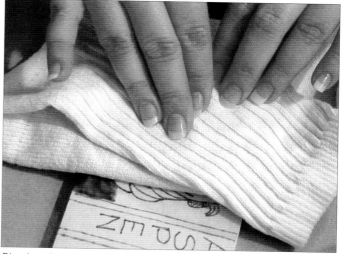
Blotting the glaze with a rag.

Painting & Glazing (cont.)

4. With a clean part of the rag, gently rub the surface to remove more of the glaze, revealing the woodburned lines. If necessary, dampen the rag slightly and remove more glaze.

5. Occasionally, during blotting or rubbing, some glaze may smear on adjacent areas. To remove it, use an ink/pencil eraser (first the ink portion, then the pencil portion). It may be necessary to use very small pieces of fine grit sandpaper, then erase with the white pencil portion of the eraser.

6. Carefully brush the second glaze color close to the finished areas, then blot and rub away from the finished portions of the design. Blotting is very important—you don't want to accidentally smear the second color into the first.

7. Occasionally, you may be instructed to **dry brush** one glaze color over another or to dry brush gold or another metallic paint over a stain. To do this, lightly load a large, dry paintbrush with paint. Blot the brush on a rag or piece of scrap paper to remove most of the paint. Brush the paint on the wood, letting the stain show through the paint.

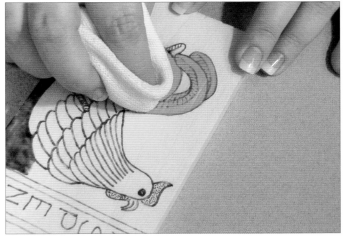

Rubbing off glaze after blotting.

Erasing smears.

Adding a second glaze color.

28

Coloring with Oil Pencils

The best pencils for adding color to woodburned designs are made with an oil pigment encased in a wax base. The pencils can be applied with light pressure to produce a soft pastel look. Medium pressure produces a little more color density. When used with heavy pressure, the maximum color and density are possible.

Most of the projects in this book use a layering method:

First layer: For the first layer of color, use light pressure and skim the pencil over the surface, indicating color but not producing a waxy finish. If desired, you can stop with this first layer and varnish the piece.

Second layer: The next layer is white pencil, applied over the colored areas with heavy pressure. This lightens the colors underneath without changing their hue and prepares the surface to accept another layer of the first color. Don't use white as the final layer—another layer of color should be applied on top of it.

Third layer: Apply the first color again, using medium pressure.

Blend oil color pencils with your fingertip, a clean rag, or a cotton swab. Blending is most effective when several layers of color have been applied.

Blow away, then wipe off any pencil debris that may have accumulated from the coloring. If it remains on the raw wood, it may smear when varnish is applied.

Continued on page 30

Applying the first layer of color with an oil pencil.

Using the white pencil to apply a second layer.

Blending colors with a cotton swab.

Oil Pencils (cont.)

CORRECTING PROBLEM AREAS

Oil color pencil can be erased if it has not been too heavily applied. Use the ink end of the eraser first, and clean up with the pencil portion of the eraser. Very fine grit sandpaper may be helpful. Be sure to gently blow away all eraser dust and sawdust.

If the woodburning lines are obscured by oil color pencil, you can carefully re-burn those areas—there are no ingredients in oil color pencils that are harmful when heated—but areas that are re-burned may be either darker or lighter than the original woodburning. If they are lighter, the woodburned design can be retouched with a burnt umber oil pencil. You also can use the burnt umber pencil to shade other oil pencil colors.

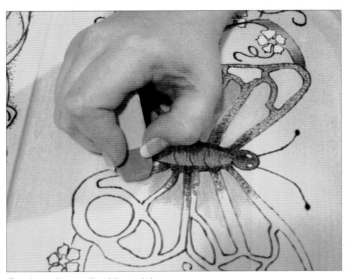

Erasing oil pencil with an ink eraser.

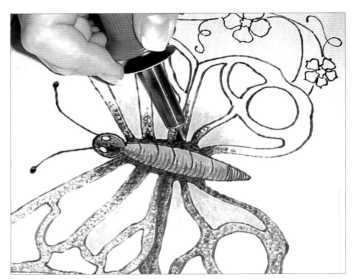

Re-burning an area that was obscured by oil color pencil.

Using a burnt umber pencil to touch up the woodburning.

Using a burnt umber pencil for shading a design.

∼ 6 ∼
Foiling

This step is optional.

Foiling can be used to trim portions of your projects. Foiling is similar to gold leafing and adds a rich metallic elegance to your projects. Supplies for foiling or gilding can be found at crafts stores. Foil comes in a variety of colors and can be selectively applied to edges, to large areas of the design, or as small accents in very tiny areas.

In this book, I've used a foiling kit that includes an adhesive that is painted on areas where the foil will be applied. When the adhesive is set, the foil is pressed, shiny side up, over the adhesive.

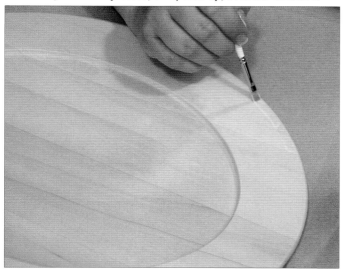

Applying foil adhesive with a brush.

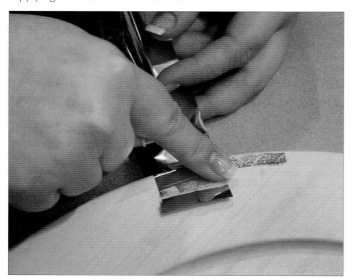

Pressing foil over the adhesive with your fingertips.

∼ 7 ∼
Finishing

When burning and coloring are complete, it's important to protect your piece with at least two coats of acrylic varnish. You may use a spray-on type or a brush-on type. Work in a well-lighted area; it can be difficult to see where you have varnished and where you have not. All parts of the wood need to be sealed to prevent warping, including the undersides of tables and the insides of boxes and drawers. You can use satin, gloss, or matte varnishes. Suggestions are included for each project to guide you in your selection.

If using colored pencils, I like to spray a coat of matte acrylic sealer on the piece. (This sets the colors and keeps them from smearing.) When sealer is dry, sand lightly and wipe away dust. Then you can spray with a second coat of sealer or apply one or two coats of brush-on varnish. The brush-on varnish has a little different look and it is thicker, providing more protection. Choose the one that is best for your piece.

∼ 8 ∼
Installing Hardware

Replacing the hardware is the final step. If you are using new pulls or handles, you may need to buy some extra screws so they'll be the proper length. Measure the thickness of the wood, and tell the salesperson at the hardware store or home improvement center what you need. You will usually receive lots of help selecting the proper screws. ❏

Projects

Once you have learned the basics of woodburning, you
are ready to create a project to use in your home or give
as a gift. The basic techniques covered in the previous
chapters are not repeated for the project instructions.
Please refer to these basic technique chapters if you have
questions about the procedure as you are creating your project.
The instructions for the projects in this book are specific
to each individual project. You may wish to substitute
surfaces or techniques once you have discovered which ones
are your favorites.

Patterns for all projects can be found at the end of the
"Projects" section of the book. Feel free to use the patterns as
you desire to create your own pieces of art. Patterns can be
enlarged, reduced, or used on different styles of wood projects
other than those shown. We have given a % of enlargement
needed to make the pattern the actual size as shown for a
specific piece of wood. If your wood is of a different style,
experiment with the size of the pattern so that it will fit
your piece of wood.

BUTTERFLY TRAY

This wooden tray has two pattern pieces —the large butterfly for the center and a border pattern with three small butterflies. The ribbon ends are freehanded and are different on each corner of the tray. This tray can be used as a food serving tray or as a tray to hold perfumes. I like to use mine in my guest room to hold bottled water and some night time chocolates for overnight guests. You will want to apply a good varnish to the tray to protect it so that you will feel free to use the tray and impress your company.

YOU'LL NEED

Wooden Piece:
Large basswood Chippendale-style tray, approximately 12" x 16"

Woodburning Tools:
Woodburner with flow point and mini-flow point
Workspace set-up supplies

Oil Color Pencils:
White, Deco blue, Cream, Light blue, Yellow, Parrot green, Orange, Olive green, Scarlet red, Burnt umber
Electric or battery-operated pencil sharpener

Finish:
Matte sealer spray or Satin varnish

Other Tools & Supplies:
1" foam brush *or* 3/4" flat white bristle paintbrush
General supplies as listed in "Supplies" chapter

HERE'S HOW

Preparation:
1. Sand tray.
2. Trace and transfer the large butterfly to the center of the tray, adding the ribbons and flowers at each side.
3. Trace and transfer the smaller butterflies around one corner. Repeat on the opposite corner.
4. Complete the border design. With a pencil, add some curving ribbon tails, ending them near the corners. If you aren't confident about drawing the ribbons, draw them on tracing paper first, then transfer.

Woodburning:
This project is used for illustration of the pencil techniques in the "Coloring With Oil Pencils" section; use those photos for reference.

1. Prepare and heat woodburner.
2. Outline all designs with the flow point.
3. Add details with the mini-flow point.
4. Switch back to the flow point and create variations in the thickness and darkness of some of the lines to add interest.
5. With the mini-flow point, fill in the dark areas, referring to the photo for placement.
6. With the flow point or mini-flow point, lightly stipple the backgrounds, letting the dots fade out as they get farther away from the designs.
7. Erase pencil and transfer marks.

Coloring:
Color the designs with oil color pencils.
1. Blossoms - Use medium to heavy pressure to color all flowers white and their centers yellow.
2. Large butterfly body - With medium to heavy pressure, color

the body olive green, then blend with cream and add a layer of parrot green.

3. Large butterfly wings - Use a combination of deco blue, light blue, and parrot green blended with white to color the various areas on the butterfly wings. Make the wings mirror images of each other when choosing the colors—use the same colors and layers on the same areas of each wing. Layer lightly with a color, layer heavily with white, then repeat the same color over the white, using medium to heavy pressure.

4. Small butterflies - Color all the white areas, using medium to heavy pressure. Then color each butterfly with one of the three colors you used on the large butterfly. Use light to medium pressure. Blend with cotton swabs.

5. Ribbons - Using medium to heavy pressure, color the darker areas of ribbon with scarlet red and the remainder with orange. Then blend with cream. Add some more layers of orange and red over the cream if needed to make the colors

deep and rich. *Option:* Blend some yellow into the ribbons around the rim of the tray.

6. Blow away, then wipe off any pencil debris that may have accumulated from the coloring. If it remains on the raw wood, it may smear when varnish is applied.

Touching Up:
If the woodburning has been obscured by the color pencils, burn over the areas once more or color them with burnt umber pencil to darken them.

Finishing:
1. Spray the entire tray, back and front, with sealer. Let dry.
2. Sand lightly. Wipe away dust.
3. Spray with a second coat of sealer. *Option:* If you like the look of brushed on varnish, apply one or two coats. ❏

PEARLY DRAGONFLY CHEST

This versatile design can be used on many different furniture pieces. I started with a four-door cabinet and removed the lower doors so the bottom part is an open shelf. This very easy project is recommended for beginners.

HERE'S HOW

Preparation:
1. Remove the knobs from doors.
2. Sand cabinet edges and surfaces.
3. Trace and transfer dragonflies to cabinet.
4. With a pencil, add some looping lines to indicate flight paths behind the dragonflies on the top, bringing them over the front edge and down onto the doors. Add some flight paths behind the dragonflies on the doors.

Woodburning:
1. Prepare and heat woodburner.
2. Outline dragonflies with the mini-flow point and add details on the wings and bodies.
3. Switch to the flow point and burn the flight paths, creating variations in the thickness and darkness of some of the lines.
4. Erase pencil and transfer marks.

Coloring:
When mixed with mediums, the paint colors will be much lighter than they are in the bottle. Adjust the amounts to get the colors you desire.
1. Mix the colors for the dragonflies:
   • One tablespoon pearlizing medium to three drops purple
   • One tablespoon pearlizing medium to three drops green
   • One tablespoon pearlizing medium to three drops burgundy
   Paint the wings with variations of the three colors, not allowing them to mix together on the wood. Blot each color before applying the next. Refer to the project photo for color placement.
2. Blot up all excess glaze.
3. Slightly dampen a rag and rub off as much color as desired.
4. Apply two coats of satin varnish to the **dragonflies only**, not the background. Let dry.

YOU'LL NEED
Wooden Piece:
Small 4-door pine cabinet

Woodburning Tools:
Woodburner with flow point and mini-flow point
Workspace set-up supplies

Acrylic Paints & Mediums:
Neutral Glazing medium
Pearlizing medium
Acrylic Paints:
    Medium green
    Dioxazine purple
    True burgundy
    Burnt sienna

Finish:
Satin acrylic varnish

Other Tools & Supplies:
Satin varnish
General supplies as listed in "Supplies" chapter
3/4" flat white bristle paintbrush
1/2" flat sable brush
Small round paintbrush
Screwdriver
White ceramic knobs with screws

Staining:
1. Mix three parts neutral glazing medium and one part burnt sienna. Prepare enough stain to cover the top and the doors.
2. Rub the stain on the cabinet top and doors. Take care not to obscure the dragonflies. Be sure to stain the edges of the top.
3. Mix medium green paint with a little glazing medium to make a transparent stain. Brush on the remaining areas of the cabinet, inside and out. Don't rub it down. Let dry.

Finishing:
1. Apply two coats satin varnish to the entire cabinet, inside and out. Let dry and sand between coats.
2. Replace wooden knobs with white ceramic ones. ❏

RUSTIC LILIES BENCH

This project uses a technique similar to the methods used by our Victorian ancestors for achieving a deep, dark, rich brown coloration. They used a mahogany stain over the darkly burned areas to even out the burning and produce gorgeous color. That's why many antique woodburned pieces appear so faded. The stain has disappeared over time, but the burning has remained.

Instructions follow on next page

YOU'LL NEED

Wooden Piece:
Medium-size pine pantry bench

Woodburning Tools:
Woodburner with flow point and shading point
Workspace set-up supplies

Acrylic Paints & Mediums:
Neutral glazing medium
Acrylic Paints: Asphaltum, Light green, Portrait, Pure gold, Turner's yellow

Finish:
Satin varnish

Other Tools & Supplies:
3/4" flat white bristle paintbrush
1/2" flat sable paintbrush
Small round artist's paintbrush
General supplies as listed in "Supplies" chapter

HERE'S HOW

Preparation:
1. Sand bench edges and surfaces. Wipe away dust.
2. Trace and transfer lilies to bench top and at least one side of the brace.

Woodburning:
The woodburning techniques used on this bench are outlining and shading.
1. Prepare and heat woodburner.
2. Outline lilies, leaves, and stems with the flow point. Add details.
3. Switch to the shading point and burn the background around the designs a solid, dark brown.
4. Erase pencil and transfer marks.

Coloring:
When mixed with glazing medium, the paint colors will be much lighter than they are in the bottle. Adjust the amount of paint or glaze to get the color you desire.
1. Mix the colors for the lilies and leaves:
   • One tablespoon glazing medium to three drops Turner's yellow

   • One tablespoon glazing medium to three drops light green
   • One tablespoon glazing medium to three drops portrait
2. Paint the lilies with portrait mix, then blot. Add a few strokes of Turner's yellow mix to the center of each lily, moving toward the tips of the petals. Blot.
3. Paint the leaves and stems with light green mix.
4. Blot up all excess glaze.
5. Slightly dampen a rag and rub off as much color as desired.
6. Paint the stamen with Turner's yellow paint (no glazing medium), using a small round paintbrush.

Staining:

Staining helps even out the color of woodburned areas and deepens its intensity. Apply it to the deeply burned sections on the top of the bench and the brace.

1. Mix three parts glazing medium and one part asphaltum to make the mahogany stain. Prepare enough stain to cover the entire area where you used the shading point.
2. Paint the stain on a 4-5" area of the background at a time. Try not to get it on the flowers and leaves. Blot each section as you work to remove all excess stain. Let dry.

Finishing:

1. Paint the edges of the top and the legs of the bench with two coats of gold paint. Let dry between coats.
2. When the second coat of paint is dry, apply two coats satin varnish to the entire bench. Let dry and sand between coats.
❑

LEAFY PLANT TABLE

When I bought this table, it wasn't assembled. It was easier to work on in pieces, so I assembled it after I applied the varnish.

Instructions follow on page 44

See photo also on pages 42 & 43.

HERE'S HOW

Preparation:
1. Sand table edges and surfaces. Wipe away dust.
2. Trace and transfer the leaf section of the pattern to each of the four corners of the tabletop.
3. Use a pencil and ruler to draw the borders all around the table, skipping over the leaves so they appear to lay over the borders.
4. With a pencil and a ruler, lightly draw diagonal lines to create the barber pole striping all around the tabletop on the border that frames the center of the table. Skip over the leaves.
5. Transfer a medallion design to the center of the band on each side of the tabletop. See photos for placement.
6. Transfer a medallion design to the center of each piece of the apron.

Woodburning:
In addition to outlining, the woodburning techniques used on this project are dots, fill-in, and shading.
1. Prepare and heat woodburner.
2. With the flow point, outline all design elements, including leaves, medallions, and straight lines to create the bands.
3. Add curving lines and veins on the leaves. Create variations in the thickness and darkness of some of the lines to add interest and avoid sameness.
4. Still using the flow point, darken the wide background band with fill-in movements.
5. Make a row of dots along the outermost narrow band. Hold the woodburner upright, and touch the entire rounded point to the wood so a perfectly round dot is formed. Lift and make the next one. If needed, make pencil marks every 1/4" to guide you in evenly spacing the dots.
6. Add the details and fill-in areas on the medallions.
7. Switch to the shading point to create the shadows on the leaves and add darker areas behind the top leaves to cast shadows on the leaves beneath them.
8. Erase pencil and transfer marks.

YOU'LL NEED

Wooden Piece:
Hardwood plant table or end table

Woodburning Tools:
Woodburner with flow point, mini-flow point, and shading point
Workspace set-up supplies

Acrylic Paints & Mediums:
Neutral glazing medium
Acrylic Paints:
Burnt sienna
Light red oxide
Pale metallic gold

Finish:
Satin varnish

Other Tools & Supplies:
3/4" flat white bristle paintbrush
1/2" flat sable paintbrush
Small round paintbrush
General supplies as listed in "Supplies" chapter

Staining:
1. Mix equal amounts light red oxide and burnt sienna.
2. Add one part of the mix to three parts glazing medium to make a honey maple stain.
3. Brush this stain on two legs and rub off.
4. Use the same technique to stain the apron, avoiding the medallions. Leave them unstained.

Painting:
1. Paint the edges of the tabletop with pale gold acrylic paint, bringing it up around the edges just to the first band which frames the design. *Option:* Paint the edges of the apron and the legs with pale gold.
2. Dry brush some pale gold over the stain on the skirting panels. Let dry.

Finishing:
1. Apply two coats satin varnish. Let dry and sand between coats.
2. Assemble the table. ❑

TULIP LYRE-BACK CHAIR

This chair was purchased from an unfinished furniture store. It's made of parawood from Malaysia. Parawood is a lovely, even, dense hardwood that burns beautifully. Because of the chair's size, there are several pieces to the pattern. The small stylized tulip is transferred to three places on the seat. The design is accented with gold foil.

YOU'LL NEED

Wooden Piece:
Unfinished hardwood chair with lyre back

Woodburning Tools:
Woodburner with flow point
Workspace set-up supplies

Acrylic Paints & Mediums:
Neutral glazing medium
Acrylic Paints:
 Raw sienna
 Turner's yellow
 Yellow light

Finishes:
Matte varnish

Other Tools & Supplies:
Gold foil and adhesive
3/4" flat white bristle paintbrush
1/2" flat white sable paintbrush
Small round paintbrush
General supplies as listed in "Supplies" chapter

HERE'S HOW

Preparation:
1. Sand lightly with the grain. Remove dust.
2. Trace and transfer the designs. Place the small stylized flower on the center front of the apron and at the front corners of the chair seat.

Woodburning:
The woodburning techniques used on this project are fill-in, circles, and parallel lines.
1. Prepare and heat woodburner.
2. With the flow point, outline all design elements, including ribbons, stylized flowers, and straight bands. Add details.
3. Cover the insides of the wood on the chair back as necessary with two layers of masking tape to protect them from accidental burns.
4. Using photo as a guide, burn the backgrounds using the fill-in technique, varying the darkness in some areas to add interest.
5. Add parallel lines to the stylized flowers and other design areas. Fill some sections of the stylized flowers with circles to create texture and contrast within the design. Add details to the three flowers on the seat and apron.
6. Erase all pencil and transfer marks. Wipe away any dust.

Continued on page 48

(instructions continued from page 46)

Coloring:

The dense surface of this chair required a mix of equal amounts of paint and glaze. Other woods may not require quite as much pigment; test your mixes on a spot where they will not show, such as underneath the seat, and adjust as necessary.

1. Mix the colors:
   • One part glazing medium to one part yellow light
   • One part glazing medium to one part Turner's yellow
   • One part glazing medium to one part raw sienna
2. Paint the petals of the all stylized flowers with the yellow light mix. Blot the color.
3. Paint the ribbon banner with the Turner's yellow mix. Blot.
4. Paint over the scribbled background with the raw sienna mix. Blot.
5. Slightly dampen a rag and rub off as much color as desired.

Gold Foiling:

Add gold foil to the edges of the chair seat, to the edge across the top of the chair, and to the bar that holds the spindles in the chair back, following manufacturer's instructions.

Finishing:

Apply two coats of matte varnish. Allow to dry and sand between coats. Varnish the spindles, the undersides, and other unseen areas, too, so the wood will not warp. ❏

See photo of entire chair on page 47.

BOWL OF ACORNS

This bowl could hold nuts, salad, bread or muffins, or today's mail. If the bowl is to be used for serving food, you'll need to use a non-toxic, food-safe finish as I did here instead of varnish.

Instructions follow on next page.

YOU'LL NEED

Wooden Piece:
Round oak or maple bowl, 11-1/2"
    diameter

Woodburning Tools:
Woodburner with flow point
Workspace set-up supplies

Finish:
Mineral oil or other food-safe finish

Other Tools & Supplies:
Tissue paper
General supplies as listed in "Supplies"
    chapter

HERE'S HOW

Preparation:
1. Sand inside of bowl with fine sandpaper. Remove dust.
2. The pattern is provided in sections. Trace it on tissue paper, including the line of the top edge of the bowl, to help in placing of the design. The tissue paper bends easily on the curved surface and makes the transfer easier.
3. Transfer the tracing four times around the inside of the bowl.

Woodburning:
In addition to outlining, the woodburning technique used is stippling.
1. Prepare and heat woodburner.
2. With the flow point, outline all design elements, including acorns, leaves, and twigs. Create variations in the thickness and darkness of some of the lines to add interest. Add shading and texture lines on the acorns.
3. Switch to the mini-flow point and stipple the shadows on the leaves. Add some stippling to the twigs for texture.
4. Go back over the stippling with either of the two points to darken some areas more than others.
5. Erase pencil and transfer marks.

Finishing:
Rub on several coats of mineral oil or other food-safe sealer. Let dry between coats. ❏

Harvest Bread Board

This decorated bread board will look wonderful hanging on your kitchen wall. If you want to use the back for cutting bread or chopping vegetables, use a food-safe finish and do not varnish the back. A combination of oil pencil and colored glaze is used to achieve the subtle shading on the wheat heads.

Here's How

Preparation:
1. Sand edges and surfaces with the grain of the wood. Remove dust.
2. Trace and transfer design to cutting board. Be sure to put the design on the side with the beveled edges, so the back remains flat. The back will be the cutting and serving surface, and will lie against the wall or the counter.

Woodburning:
1. Prepare and heat the woodburner.
2. Outline all parts of the design with the mini-flow point.
3. Add details on the leaves and wheat heads.
4. Switch to the flow point and burn the rows of dots around the design.
5. Draw a pencil line along the top edge of the board where it slants and begins to be beveled for the handle, using photo as a guide. Burn a row of dots along this line.
6. Erase all pencil and transfer marks.

Coloring:
1. Use an oil pencil to color the right half of each upright wheat head with canary yellow. Color the remainder with yellow. Use medium to heavy pressure.
2. For the two wheat heads lying across the top of the design, color the bottom half with canary yellow and the remainder with yellow. Use medium to heavy pressure.
3. Begin coloring at the base of each leaf with olive green using light to medium pressure, going up about a third to a half of

You'll Need

Wooden Piece:
Hardwood bread and pizza board (sometimes referred to as a "peel")

Woodburning Tools:
Woodburner with flow point and mini-flow point
Workspace set-up supplies

Acrylic Paints & Mediums:
Neutral glazing medium
Acrylic Paints: Burnt sienna

Oil Color Pencils:
Burnt sienna
Canary yellow
Light green
Olive green
Yellow

Finishes:
Satin varnish
Matte sealer spray
Mineral oil or other food-safe finish

Other Tools & Supplies:
3/4" flat white bristle paintbrush
General supplies as listed in "Supplies" chapter

the way. Vary the amount of olive green on each leaf for variety.
4. Finish the leaves with light green, using medium to hard pressure.
5. Blend the colors with a cotton swab.
6. Color the stems with light green.
7. Color the bottom half or so of each letter of the word "Bread" with burnt sienna, using light to medium pressure.
8. Finish each letter with canary yellow, using heavy pressure.
9. Blend with a cotton swab.
10. Color the center of each scroll in the border around the word lightly with burnt sienna, then apply canary yellow and blend with a cotton swab.

Continued on page 56

(instructions continued from page 54)

Painting:

Paint the handle and the top section of the board with two coats of burnt sienna acrylic paint.

Adding Shadows with Glaze:

1. Mix a tablespoon of glazing medium with three drops of burnt sienna paint.
2. Dip a rag into the mixture. Rub the rag together to minimize the amount of glaze on it. Wrap a portion of the rag around your finger and carefully rub it along the wheat heads, close to the right side of each one. Leave a little yellow along the edge, and create a shadow slightly in from the edge. See photo for placement. Let dry.

Finishing:

1. Rub several coats of mineral oil or other food-safe sealer on the plain (back) side of the board. Let dry between coats.
2. Brush the woodburned side of the board, including the handle, with at least two coats of satin varnish. Let dry and sand between coats. ❏

Sweet Teapot Napkin Holder

This very easy project is recommended for beginners. The smaller scroll at the top of the design is repeated on the lid and on the cup.

You'll Need

Wooden Piece:
Pine teapot-shaped napkin holder

Woodburning Tools:
Woodburner with flow point
Workspace set-up supplies

Acrylic Paints & Mediums:
Neutral glazing medium
Acrylic Paint: Titanium white

Finish: Satin varnish

Other Tools & Supplies:
1/2" flat sable brush
3/4" flat white bristle brush
General supplies as listed in "Supplies" chapter

Here's How

Preparation:

1. Sand napkin holder. Remove dust.
2. Trace and transfer the larger motif to the front of the teapot, referring to the photo for placement.
3. Trace the smaller scroll on a separate piece of tracing paper. Transfer it to the teapot lid and to the top edge of the cup.
4. Trace 1/2" scallops and transfer around the knob, spout, and handles. See photo for placement.

Woodburning:

The woodburning techniques used on this project are outlining and dots.

1. Prepare and heat woodburner.
2. With the flow point, outline all design elements and burn the scallops.

3. Add dots in the center of each scallop.
4. With a pencil, draw two parallel, curving pencil lines around the neck of the teapot, 1" or less apart. Draw parallel lines to connect them. See photo for placement.
5. Burn over these guidelines with the flow point.
6. Erase all pencil and transfer marks. Wipe away dust.

Coloring:

1. Mix 1 tablespoon of glazing medium with an equal amount of titanium white paint.

2. Working one area at a time, brush glaze mix on the handles, spout, and knob, then blot.
3. Rub off some of the glaze with a damp rag.
4. Use titanium white paint (without glazing medium) to fill in the three teardrop accents on each design. Let dry.

Finishing:

Apply at least two coats of satin varnish. Allow to dry and sand between coats. ❏

COOK'S TOOL KIT

What a wonderful way to personalize a gift. Replace the word "Cook's" with the person's name. This is an especially appropriate gift to give a man—especially if he doesn't wear ties. The easy vine pattern can be adapted to any size knife handle or wooden block.

HERE'S HOW

Preparation:
1. Sand butcher block and all tool handles, being sure to sand away any sealer or other finish that may be present on these items. If you don't you'll release noxious fumes when you woodburn.
2. Using photo as a guide, trace and transfer the pattern to the block.
3. Transfer the vine part of the pattern to the tool handles.

Woodburning:
1. Prepare and heat woodburner.
2. Outline designs with the mini-flow point.
3. Add a central vein to each leaf. Add a few wavy lines to the words for texture. If the wood is particularly hard, you may need to reinforce the lines with the flow point, which will burn

YOU'LL NEED

Wooden Pieces:
Hardwood knife block with wooden-handled tools

Woodburning Tools:
Woodburner with mini-flow point and optional flow point
Workspace set-up supplies

Oil Color Pencils:
Blue green
Bright green
Dark brown
Green
Olive green

Finishes:
Matte acrylic sealer spray
Optional: Matte or satin varnish

Other Tools & Supplies:
3/4" flat white bristle paintbrush
General supplies as listed in "Supplies" chapter

darker but not with as much small detail.
4. Erase pencil and transfer marks.

Coloring:
Color the designs with the colored pencils. Vary the greens on all the leaves on the block and on the tools using a light and a dark on each leaf. Use the photo as a guide.

Finishing:
1. Spray with matte sealer. Let dry.
2. Apply at least two coats of satin varnish to all the wood surfaces. Allow to dry and sand between coats. ❑

FANTASY FLOWERS TRAY

This project looks difficult, but it's really one of the easier ones—almost all the woodburning is outlining, and the color is added with oil pencils, which are as easy to use as crayons.

Instructions follow on page 62

See photo on pages 60-61.

YOU'LL NEED

Wooden Piece:
Large basswood Chippendale-style tray,
   12" x 16"

Woodburning Tools:
Woodburner with flow point and
   mini-flow point
Workspace set-up supplies

Oil Color Pencils:

Blue green	Indigo blue
Blue slate	Lavender
Blush pink	Lemon yellow
Bright green	Light blue
Deco blue	Periwinkle
Green	Purple
Greyed lavender	White
Hot pink	Yellow
Imperial violet	Yellow orange

Finishes:
Matte acrylic sealer spray
Optional: Matte or satin varnish

Other Tools & Supplies:
3/4" flat white bristle paintbrush
General supplies as listed in "Supplies" chapter

HERE'S HOW

Preparation:
1. Sand tray and remove dust.
2. Trace the flower spray and transfer the flowers to one corner of the tray, then repeat on the opposite corner.
3. With No. 2 pencil, add some curving ribbons, looping them over and under each other until they reach almost to the corners. If you aren't confident about drawing these ribbons, do them on tracing paper first, then transfer as for any other pattern. *Refer to the photos for placement.*

Woodburning:
The techniques used on this project are outlining and stippling.

1. Prepare and heat woodburner.
2. Outline flowers, leaves, stems, and ribbons with the flow point.
3. Add details with the mini-flow point.
4. Switch back to the flow point and create variations in the thickness and darkness of some of the lines to add interest.
5. With the flow point, lightly stipple the areas around the designs, letting the dots fade out as they get farther away from the flowers.
6. Stipple lightly in each corner on the inside bottom of the tray.
7. Erase pencil and transfer marks.

Coloring:
1. Blossoms with backs turned - Color lightly around the petal edges with blush pink, covering about a third of each petal. Then color out from the stem area with imperial violet, varying the amount of pink and violet on each petal. Add some blue violet at the very base of the petal. Blend all the colors with a heavy coat of white. Use a cotton swab to blend further.
2. Open blooms - Make two blooms of each shade of blue, two purple, and two blue violet, using these colors:
Blue flowers #1- yellow, indigo blue, blue slate, light blue, white.
Blue flowers #2- yellow, indigo blue, deco blue, periwinkle, white.
Purple flowers - yellow orange, purple, blush pink, hot pink, white.
Blue violet flowers - yellow orange, lavender, greyed lavender, white.
3. Stems, leaves & tendrils - blue green, green, bright green, lemon yellow.
4. Background - Lightly color around the edges of the tray outside the flowers with deco blue and blend with a heavy layer of white. Continue layering these two colors until even. Blend with clean rag or cotton swab.
5. Color lightly over the stippled woodburning (shadows) with imperial violet.

Finishing:
Spray the entire tray, back and front, with two coats of matte sealer. Allow to dry and sand between coats. If you like the look of brushed on varnish, add one or two coats. ❏

SHELL KEEPER BOX

*The shells are colored, then varnished, before glazing the rest of the box,
to keep them from being stained by the glaze.*

YOU'LL NEED

Wooden Piece:
Small, round wooden box with lid (imported
   soft wood, approx. 2-1/2" diameter)

Woodburning Tools:
Woodburner with mini-flow point
Workspace set-up supplies

Acrylic Paints & Medium:
Neutral glazing medium
Acrylic Paint: Aqua

Oil Color Pencil: White

Finish: Satin varnish

Other Tools & Supplies:
3/4" flat white bristle paintbrush
General supplies as listed in "Supplies" chapter

HERE'S HOW

Preparation:
1. With fine sandpaper, sand lightly with the grain, paying close attention to curves and lightly rounding off sharp edges.
2. Trace the pattern and tape lightly around the box, leaving room for the circle.
3. With a pencil, connect the wavy lines where the patterns meet.
4. Transfer the circle and pencil a fat initial in the middle of it.
5. Transfer the large shell to the top of the box.

Woodburning:
The woodburning techniques used in this project are outlining, dots, and fill-in.
1. Prepare and heat woodburner.
2. With the mini-flow point, outline all design elements.
3. Burn two rows of dots around the edges of the lid, referring to photo for placement.
4. Erase all pencil and transfer marks, and wipe away any dust.

Coloring:
1. Using heavy pressure, color all the shells with the white pencil. Brush away any pencil debris.
2. Brush the shells only with two coats of varnish. Let dry.
3. Mix one tablespoon glazing medium and one tablespoon aqua paint. Apply to the lid. (You can brush it right over the shell.) Blot immediately. (The varnish will protect the shell.)
4. Apply aqua mix to upper and lower bands on box base.
5. Add another tablespoon of glazing medium to the remaining aqua mix and paint the center band on the box base, blotting each shell as you go.
6. Paint inside the box and lid with aqua (no glazing medium). Let dry.

Finishing:
Apply at least two coats of satin varnish to the box, inside and out. Let dry and sand between coats. ❑

VIVID CANDLE BOX

This very easy project is recommended for beginners. I've used a crimson glaze, but you could paint the inside of the box or the edges or lid with metallic paint or a burnt sienna glaze mixture. This box lends itself to experimentation and is a good project for trying new things. You also could add some hardware to the front of this box, such as a knob or a clasp. Have fun with it!

YOU'LL NEED

Wooden Piece:
Basswood candle box

Woodburning Tools:
Woodburner with flow point
Workspace set-up supplies

Acrylic Medium:
Neutral glazing medium
Acrylic Paint, Alizarin crimson

Finish:
Satin or gloss varnish

Other Tools & Supplies:
3/4" flat white bristle paintbrush
General supplies as listed in "Supplies" chapter

HERE'S HOW

Preparation:
1. With fine sandpaper, sand lightly with the grain. Remove dust.
2. Mark narrow 3/16" bands around the edge of the lid and around the top of the box base. Lightly draw diagonal lines to create the barber pole striping all around the lid.
3. Trace and transfer the leaf design to the lid, using photo as a guide for placement.

Woodburning:
This project uses the outlining and fill-in techniques.
1. Prepare and heat woodburner.
2. Burn the stylized leaves with the flow point.

3. Fill in the stripes on the band on the lid.
4. Fill in the band at the top of the box base.
5. Erase all pencil and transfer marks.

Coloring:
1. Mix equal amounts of alizarin crimson and neutral glazing medium. Brush on the lid and wipe off.
2. Apply glaze mix to the inside and edges of the box and lid. Let dry.

Finishing:
Apply two coats of varnish to the entire box, inside and out. Let dry and sand between coats. ❏

VICTORIAN PHOTO ALBUM

For this project, you will need a photograph or an old postcard that can be photocopied and sized to fit the opening on the pattern with arched areas at the top and the bottom. Use the one provided on page 75 or choose your own.

YOU'LL NEED

Wooden Piece:
Basswood photo album with 8-1/2" x 11" pages

Woodburning Tools:
Woodburner with mini-flow point
Workspace set-up supplies

Acrylic Paints & Medium:
Neutral Glazing medium
Acrylic Paints:
    Dove grey
    Portrait beige

Oil Color Pencils:
Green
White
Yellow

Finish:
Satin varnish

Other Tools & Supplies:
Decoupage medium
3/4" flat white bristle paintbrush
Clean, soft, lint-free rag
Wax paper or plastic wrap
Photocopy of photograph or postcard, sized to
    fit opening
Screwdriver
General supplies as listed in "Supplies" chapter

HERE'S HOW

Preparation:

1. Use a screwdriver to remove the brass screws that hold the front and back of the album together. Set them aside, separating the cover piece to decorate. Leave the hinges attached.
2. With fine sandpaper, sand lightly with the grain. Remove dust.
3. Trace and transfer design, centering on front of album cover.

Woodburning:

The woodburning techniques used on this project are outlining, dots, fill-in, and wavy lines.

1. Prepare and heat woodburner.
2. Outline all design elements, switching between the flow point and the mini-flow point to burn the lines darkly.
3. Use the mini-flow point to add details on the flowers, leaves, branches, and other elements. Fill-in and wavy lines may be done with either point.
4. Using the photo as a guide, add detail and texture to the branches, birdhouse, flowers, and band behind the letters.
5. To make the scalloped lines, use the ruler to mark lightly every 1/2" along the line where the scallops will go, then burn half-circles to join the marks. Make a dot where the half-circles meet.
6. Erase all pencil and transfer marks. Wipe away any dust.

Coloring:

1. Mix four tablespoons of glazing medium with two teaspoons each of dove grey and portrait beige paint, stirring lightly so the mix will have a variegated look when painted.
2. Brush the mix on all album surfaces except the center space.
3. Rub off excess glaze mix. This will blend the two colors but give a mottled look. Remember to apply glaze to the back and inside the covers.
4. Dampen a rag and rub off more of the color on and around the design elements. The leaves and flowers should have just a mist of color. (If the glaze is too thick, the pencils may not cover it.) Let the glaze dry completely.

Continued on page 74

(instructions continued from page 72)

5. Use oil color pencils with light to medium pressure to color the flowers white, the leaves and stems green, and the word "Album" yellow. Add color to other design elements as desired.

Decoupaging:
1. Cover your work area with wax paper or taped down plastic wrap.
2. Use the template provided to size and cut out a photocopy of your chosen photograph or postcard (or use one from this book).

3. Place the photocopied photograph face down on the wax paper or plastic wrap and brush a coat of decoupage medium on the back.
4. Carefully turn it face up and position on the album. Smooth lightly with your fingertips from the center outward. Let dry.
5. Apply a coat of decoupage medium to album front. Let dry.

Finishing:
1. Brush the entire album, inside and out, including the photograph, with two coats of satin varnish. Let dry and sand between coats.
2. Insert album pages and re-attach the cover. ❏

You may use any of these images to photocopy and decoupage onto your album cover.
Or use one of your own photographs or antique postcards.

LEAVES & CIRCLES PHOTO ALBUM

For this album, you will need a photograph that can be photocopied and sized to approximately 4" x 6". A color photocopy of a black and white photo works well.

HERE'S HOW

Preparation:
1. Use a screwdriver to remove the brass screws that hold the album front and back together and set them aside, separating the cover piece to decorate. Leave the hinges attached.
2. With fine sandpaper, sand lightly with the grain. Wipe away dust.
3. Trace and transfer the patterns to the cover and the spine.

Woodburning:
The woodburning techniques used on this project are outlining, fill-in, and wavy lines.
1. Prepare and heat woodburner.
2. With the flow point, go over all the lines indicating the border and the bands. Outline all the circles.
3. Use the fill-in technique to darken the edges of the blank center space for about 3/4" to 1" in around all four sides. Lay the photograph temporarily in place and burn more of the background, if necessary.
4. Fill in the bands around all the circles.
5. Erase all pencil and transfer marks, Wipe away any dust.

Staining:
1. Mix four tablespoons of glazing medium with two teaspoons of light red oxide and two teaspoons of burnt sienna paint, stirring well.
2. Brush on all album surfaces except the blank center space with the glaze mix, then rub off excess. Remember to stain the album back as well as the insides. Let dry.

Painting:
Using the small, round paintbrush, paint the small circles with gold paint. Let dry.

YOU'LL NEED

Wooden Piece:
Birch album with 8-1/2" x 11" pages

Woodburning Tools:
Woodburner with flow point
Workspace set-up supplies

Acrylic Paints & Medium:
Neutral glazing medium
Acrylic Paints:
  Light red oxide
  Burnt sienna
  Pure gold metallic

Finish:
Satin varnish

Other Tools & Supplies:
Decoupage medium
3/4" flat white bristle paintbrush
Small round paintbrush
Wax paper or plastic wrap
Photocopy of photograph, sized to 4" x 6"
Screwdriver
General supplies as listed in "Supplies" chapter

Decoupaging:
1. Cover your work area with wax paper or taped down plastic wrap.
2. Place the photocopied photograph face down on the wax paper or plastic wrap and brush a coat of decoupage medium on the back.
3. Carefully turn it face up and position on the album. Smooth lightly with your fingertips from the center outward. Let dry.
4. Apply another coat of decoupage medium to album front. Let dry.

Finishing:
1. Brush the entire album, inside and out, including the photograph, with two coats of satin varnish. Let dry and sand between coats.
2. Insert album pages and re-attach the cover. ❏

VICTORIAN SWEETHEART FRAME

The woodburned design on this frame is stained with colored glazes. A burnt sienna glaze is used to shade the colors. This is a traditional Victorian design and looks good with an heirloom photo in it.

HERE'S HOW

Preparation:
1. Sand frame.
2. Trace and transfer design to frame.

Woodburning:
The woodburning techniques used on this project are outlining, hatching and cross-hatching, and stippling.
1. Prepare and heat woodburner.
2. With the flow point, outline all design elements except facial features, leaf, and flower details.
3. Still using the flow point, cover the entire background with hatching, making the marks shorter and closer together around the designs and toward the center of the frame.
4. Go back over the darker areas and add cross-hatching to them.
5. Switch to the mini-flow point and add the remaining details on the face, the flower, and the leaves. Try to leave a "sparkle" of unburned wood in the eye (it can be painted later if you cover it).
6. Erase all pencil and transfer marks. Wipe away any dust.

Coloring:
When mixed with glazing medium, the colors will be much lighter than they are in the bottle. Adjust the amount of paint or glaze as needed.
1. Mix these glazes:
   - One tablespoon glazing medium and three drops portrait.
   - One tablespoon glazing medium and three drops yellow light.
   - One tablespoon glazing medium and three drops alizarin crimson.
   - One tablespoon glazing medium with three drops medium green.
   (Save the burnt sienna to mix later.)
2. Paint the face with the portrait mixture, leaving a small area of the eye unpainted. Blot excess glaze. Rub the face with a clean rag to remove some of the color. Dampen the rag slightly, if needed.

YOU'LL NEED

Wooden Piece:
Large pine frame with oval opening.
  Frame is 11" x 14"

Woodburning Tools:
Woodburner with flow point and mini-flow point
Workspace set-up supplies

Acrylic Paints & Medium:
Neutral glazing medium
Acrylic Paints:
  Alizarin crimson
  Burnt sienna
  Medium green
  Portrait beige
  Pure gold metallic
  Titanium white
  Yellow light

Finish:
Matte varnish

Other Tools & Supplies:
3/4" flat white bristle paintbrush
1/2" flat sable brush
Small round paintbrush
General supplies as listed in "Supplies" chapter
Optional: Glass to fit oval opening

3. Paint the flowers and the bud with the alizarin crimson mix. Blot. Rub off some of the color.
4. Add a couple of drops of alizarin crimson paint to the mix to darken it. Brush this mixture on the petals.
5. Paint the lips with alizarin crimson.
6. Paint the leaves and stems with the medium green mix. Blot. Rub away most of the color.
7. Paint the hair with the yellow light mix, leaving some bare wood and brushing the color on with a sweeping motion, in the direction of the waves and curls.

Staining:
When adding shadows with stain, take care not to obscure the colors, and begin lightly. You can always add a second coat of stain or add more burnt sienna to the mix.
1. Mix three parts glazing medium to one part burnt sienna. Prepare enough stain to cover the entire frame and the details.
2. Use a rag to rub a little stain on the base of each leaf, creating shadows.

3. Shade the flowers and the hair, referring to the photo for placement. Let dry.

Painting:
Paint the barrette with gold paint. Let dry.

Finishing:
1. Apply at least two coats of satin varnish, allowing to dry and sanding between coats.
2. Place a picture in the oval opening. ❏

FLOWER GARLAND CORNER SHELF

This very easy project is recommended for beginners. The pattern is repeated to create the garland. A slight bit of color is added, but this would be just as lovely without color.

Instructions follow on next page.

See photo on pages 80–81.

HERE'S HOW

Preparation:

1. Sand the top and the curved surfaces of the shelf and round off any sharp edges.
2. Trace the flower spray. Transfer it to the left side of the corner shelf. Repeat on the right side. Add one more flower at the right end.

Woodburning:

The techniques used on this project are outlining, stippling, and shading.

1. Prepare and heat woodburner.
2. Outline flowers, leaves, and stems with the flow point.
3. Add details with the mini-flow point.
4. Switch back to the flow point and create variations in the thickness and darkness of some of the lines to add interest.
5. With the flow point, lightly stipple the areas around the designs, letting the dots fade out as they get farther away from the flowers.
6. Switch to the shading point and shade the area beneath the flower spray, all the way down to the curved edge of the shelf front.
7. Erase pencil and transfer marks.

Coloring:

When mixed with glazing medium, the colors will be much lighter than they are in the bottle. Adjust the amount of paint or glaze as needed.

1. Mix the colors for the flowers and leaves:
   - One tablespoon glazing medium and three drops portrait.
   - One tablespoon glazing medium and three drops light green.
   - One tablespoon glazing medium and three drops ice blue.

YOU'LL NEED

Wooden Piece:
Medium pine corner shelf

Woodburning Tools:
Woodburner with flow point and shading point
Workspace set-up supplies

Acrylic Paints & Medium:
Neutral glazing medium
Acrylic Paints:
   Aqua
   Bronze metallic
   Ice blue
   Light green
   Portrait beige
   Titanium white

Finish:
Matte varnish

Other Tools & Supplies:
3/4" flat white bristle paintbrush
1/2" flat sable paintbrush
Small, round paintbrush
General supplies as listed in "Supplies" chapter

   - One tablespoon glazing medium, two drops aqua, and two drops titanium white.
2. Brush the four leaves and the stems with the light green mixture. Blot excess glaze. Dampen a rag and rub off some color on each leaf, creating a highlight.
3. Paint five flowers with the portrait mix. Use photo as a guide for color placement. Blot.
4. Paint some flowers with the ice blue mix. Blot.
5. Paint remaining flowers with the aqua mix.
6. Paint the edges with two coats of bronze acrylic paint. Let dry.

Finishing:

Apply at least two coats of matte varnish. Let dry and sand between coats. ❑

PEARS & CHERRIES PLAQUES

See photo on pages 84–85.

HERE'S HOW

Preparation:

1. With fine sandpaper, sand plaques lightly with the grain, paying close attention to curves around the edge and lightly rounding off sharp edges. Wipe away dust.
2. Trace and transfer designs.

Woodburning:

The woodburning techniques used on this project are outlining and stippling.

1. Prepare and heat woodburner.
2. With the flow point, outline all design elements, including fruit and leaves, banners, and words.
3. Add some veins to the leaves.
4. Add stippling around the designs on the backgrounds, darkening the areas nearest the fruit, then stipple a few shadows on the fruit and leaves.
5. Darken the small circle and leaf motifs on each side of the plaques.
6. Erase all pencil and transfer marks. Wipe away any dust.

Coloring:

When mixed with glazing medium, the colors will be much lighter than they are in the bottle. Adjust the amount of paint or glaze as needed.

1. Mix the colors:
   - One tablespoon glazing medium and three drops alizarin crimson.
   - One tablespoon glazing medium and three drops light green.
   - One tablespoon glazing medium and three drops yellow light.
2. Paint the cherries and the word "Cherries"

YOU'LL NEED

Wooden Pieces:
Two basswood plaques, 7" x 12"

Woodburning Tools:
Woodburner with flow point
Workspace set-up supplies

Acrylic Paints & Medium:
Neutral glazing medium
Acrylic Paints:
   Light green
   Yellow light
   Naphthol crimson
   Pale gold metallic

Finish:
Satin varnish

Other Tools & Supplies:
3/4" flat white bristle paintbrush
1/2" flat sable brush
Small round paintbrush
General supplies as listed in "Supplies" chapter

with the alizarin crimson mix. Blot excess glaze. Dampen a rag and rub off some color on each cherry, creating highlights.

3. Paint the pears with the yellow light mix. Blot excess glaze. Dampen a clean area of the rag and rub off some color on each one to create highlights.
4. Dip the rag in a very small amount of the crimson mix and dab it on each pear.
5. Paint the leaves, stems, and the word "Pears" with the light green mix. With the rag, dab some green on the stippled parts of the pears.
6. Paint the edges with two coats of light gold. Let dry.

Finishing:

Apply at least two coats of satin varnish. Allow to dry and sand between coats. ❑

PEARS
&
CHERRIES
PLAQUES

Instructions found on page 83

FOLK ART STAR BOXES

These boxes originated from a Victorian-era folk story about a rabbit who thought his ears were wings. He wanted to fly, but all the other animals laughed at him until he was so discouraged he almost gave up. One day, he met the king of the animals, whom he was surprised to learn was a chicken. The king told the rabbit that if he believed in himself, he could do anything. So the rabbit lifted his ears and flew to the moon, having many great adventures along the way.

See pages 88 & 89 showing individual boxes

YOU'LL NEED

Wooden Pieces:
Set of three balsa and birch star-shaped boxes

Woodburning Tools:
Woodburner with flow point
Workspace set-up supplies

Acrylic Paints & Medium:
Neutral glazing medium
Acrylic Paints:
- Alizarin crimson
- Aqua
- Bronze or copper metallic
- Burnt sienna
- Cobalt blue
- Light green
- Medium yellow
- Turner's yellow

Finish:
Satin varnish

Other Tools & Supplies:
3/4" flat white bristle paintbrush
1/2" flat white sable paintbrush
Small round paintbrush
General supplies as listed in "Supplies" chapter

HERE'S HOW

Preparation:
1. With fine sandpaper, sand lightly with the grain.
2. Trace and transfer designs to box lids.

Woodburning:
The woodburning techniques used on this project are outlining, stippling, hatching, and basket weave.
1. Prepare and heat woodburner.
2. With the flow point, outline all design elements, including animals and the frames around them.
3. Using project photos as guides, stipple or hatch the backgrounds.
4. Burn the points of the stars, using the basket weave technique.
5. Erase all pencil and transfer marks. Wipe away any dust.

Coloring:
The box bases usually burn and stain more darkly than the lids. You may wish to test and adjust the glaze colors so the lids and bases match more closely.
1. Mix the colors:
   Rabbit - Three parts glazing medium and one part aqua.
   Chicken - Three parts glazing medium and one part alizarin crimson.

Continued on page 88

(instructions continued from page 86)

Cat - Three parts glazing medium and one part Turner's yellow.

Dog - Three parts glazing medium and one part light green.

Accents - Two parts glazing medium and one part medium yellow *or* three parts glazing medium to one part cobalt blue.

2. Apply the colors, using photos as guides for placement. Blot each color before applying the next.

3. Mix equal amounts glazing medium and burnt sienna. Brush over the basketweave backgrounds on all lids. Blot excess. Slightly dampen a rag and rub off as much color as desired.

4. Paint the lid edges with bronze or copper metallic paint. Let dry.

Finishing:

Apply two coats of satin varnish inside and out. Be sure to varnish the bottoms of the boxes to prevent warping. Let dry and sand between coats. ❏

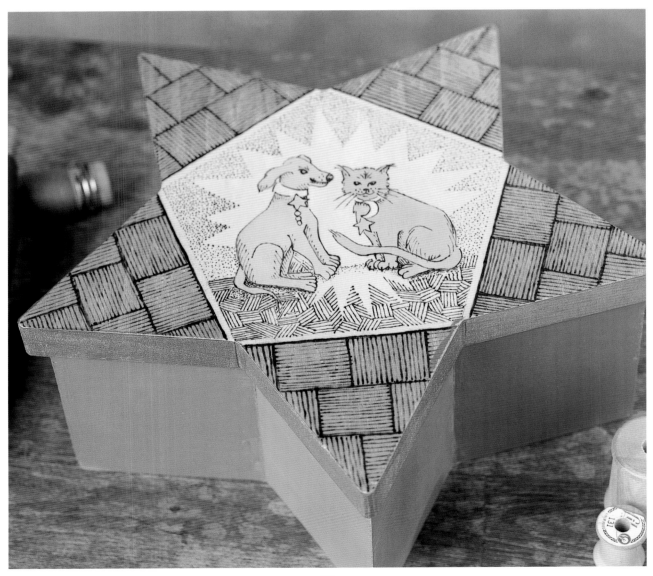

DAINTY TILTING CLOCK

This easy project is recommended for beginners. This also makes a very beautiful and useful gift.

HERE'S HOW

Preparation:
1. Sand clock frame. Wipe away dust.
2. Trace and transfer the circular leaf section of the pattern to the front of the clock frame.
3. Transfer the small leaf design to the lower left front of the base panel. Add some scrolls around the base. Refer to the photo for placement.
4. Transfer the flower design to the outside of each upright piece of the frame.

Woodburning:
The woodburning technique used on this project is outlining.
1. Prepare and heat woodburner.
2. Using the flow point, outline all design elements, including ribbons, leaves, petals, and scrolls. Add some veins to the leaves.
3. Erase all pencil and transfer marks. Wipe away any dust.

Coloring:
When mixed with glazing medium, paint colors will be much lighter than they are in the bottle. Adjust the amount of paint or glaze as needed.
1. Mix the colors for the ribbon, flowers, and leaves:
   • One tablespoon glazing medium and three drops naphthol crimson.

YOU'LL NEED

Wooden Piece:
Small tilting pine frame with oval clock bezel

Woodburning Tools:
Woodburner with flow point
Workspace set-up supplies

Acrylic Paints & Medium:
Neutral glazing medium
Acrylic Paints:
    Medium green
    Naphthol crimson

Finishes:
Satin varnish

Other Tools & Supplies:
1/2" flat sable paintbrush
Small round paintbrush
General supplies as listed in "Supplies" chapter

    • One tablespoon glazing medium and three drops medium green.
2. Paint the ribbon with crimson mix. Blot excess glaze.
3. Paint the flower petals with the crimson mix. Blot excess glaze.
4. Paint the leaves with the green mix. Blot excess glaze.
5. Slightly dampen a rag and rub off as much color as desired, creating some highlights on the ribbon. Let dry.

Finishing:
1. Apply at least two coats of satin varnish. Let dry and sand between coats.
2. Insert clock bezel into opening. ❏

ART NOUVEAU CLOCK

Stain and gold foiling accent this art nouveau–inspired clock. If the foiling kit you buy includes an antiquing medium, you can use it instead of mixing glazing medium and burnt sienna paint.

HERE'S HOW

Preparation:

1. With fine sandpaper, sand clock and base with the grain and round off sharp edges.
2. Trace and transfer designs to clock.
3. Protect the base of the clock from accidental burns by applying masking tape to cover the base where it is attached to the clock front and where it might be touched by the hot point while burning the design.

Woodburning:

The woodburning techniques used on this project are dots, fill-in, parallel lines, and shading.

1. Prepare and heat woodburner.
2. With the flow point, outline all design elements, including stylized flowers and leaves, columns, and other details.
3. Using photo as a guide, burn portions of the background with stippling.
4. In the center area around the flowers, use the fill-in technique to darken. Use the fill-in technique to darken areas around the columns.
5. Add parallel lines to the lower part of each column.
6. Switch to the shading point. Remove the masking tape from the base and apply it around the lower edge of the clock front to protect it while you burn the base.
7. Using the shading point (or the flow point and the fill-in technique), burn the top surface of the clock base a deep, dark brown.
8. Erase all pencil and transfer marks. Wipe away any dust.

Staining:

1. Use the stain that comes with the foiling kit or mix a stain with one tablespoon glazing medium and one tablespoon burnt sienna paint.

YOU'LL NEED

Wooden Piece:
Medium pine arch-style mantle clock, 11" x 7-1/2"

Woodburning Tools:
Woodburner with flow point and shading point
Workspace set-up supplies

Acrylic Paints & Medium:
Neutral glazing medium
Acrylic Paint: Burnt sienna

Finish:
Satin varnish

Other Tools & Supplies:
3-3/4" self-adhesive clock face with Roman numerals
3/8" clock movement with gold hands
Antique gold foiling kit
3/4" flat white bristle paintbrush
General supplies as listed in "Supplies" chapter

2. Wrap a clean rag around your finger, dip lightly into the stain, and blot the stain on a piece of scrap paper.
3. Apply a shadow lightly along the right side of each column, about 1/4" from the edge to suggest roundness. Rub with a clean part of the rag to soften the shadow. See photo.
4. Shade the base of each leaf and around the clock face area. Apply sparingly and refer to the photo for placement.

Adding Gold Foiling:

Add gold foil to the curved edge of the clock and the edge around the base.

Finishing:

1. Apply two coats of satin varnish. Let dry and sand between coats. Varnish the back, too, so the wood will not warp. Let dry very well.
2. Place the self-adhesive clock face on the wood, centering and making sure that it is straight and level.
3. Attach the hands. ❑

93

CANDLE SCONCES

This very easy project is recommended for beginners. Reverse the pattern for the second sconce. Since these sconces are made of fairly soft pine, they will absorb the stains and paints rather quickly. The resulting colors should be bright and clear.

HERE'S HOW

Preparation:
1. With fine sandpaper, sand lightly with the grain, paying close attention to curves around the edges. Lightly round off sharp edges.
2. Trace and transfer designs to sconces. Be sure to flip the tracing over to transfer the second one so they will be mirror images of each other rather than identical.

Woodburning:
The woodburning techniques used on this project are outlining, fill-in, stippling, and circles.
1. Prepare and heat woodburner.
2. With the flow point, outline all design elements.
3. Add stippling or fill in to darken the areas nearest the ribbons and flowers.
4. Add curving detail lines radiating out from the centers of the flowers toward the tips of the petals.
5. Add a few veins to each leaf. Make small circles in the centers of the flowers.
6. Erase all pencil and transfer marks, and wipe away any dust.

Coloring:
1. Mix the colors:
   • One tablespoon glazing medium and one tablespoon naphthol crimson.
   • One teaspoon glazing medium and one teaspoon true burgundy.
   • One teaspoon glazing medium and one teaspoon Turner's yellow.
   • One teaspoon glazing medium and one teaspoon dark green.
2. Paint the flower petals with the crimson mix. Blot excess glaze.
3. Brush some burgundy mix from the center about halfway out, curving along each petal. Blot excess glaze.
4. Paint the ribbon with the yellow mix. Blot excess.
5. Paint the leaves with the green mix. Blot excess.
6. Slightly dampen a rag and rub off as much color as desired.
7. Pick up a small amount of Turner's yellow (no glazing

YOU'LL NEED

Wooden Pieces:
Two pine decorator candle sconces, approx. 6" x 12"

Woodburning Tools:
Woodburner with flow point
Workspace set-up supplies

Acrylic Paints & Medium:
Neutral glazing medium
Acrylic Paints:
   Burnt sienna
   Burnt umber
   Dark green
   Naphthol crimson
   True burgundy
   Turner's yellow

Finish:
Satin varnish

Other Tools & Supplies:
3/4" flat white bristle paintbrush
1/2" flat sable brush
Small round paintbrush
General supplies as listed in "Supplies" chapter

medium) and paint the flower centers. Let dry.

Staining:
1. Mix four tablespoons glazing medium and two tablespoons burnt sienna to make a light stain.
2. Brush light stain around the designs. Blot, then rub away from the colored areas to avoid smears.
3. Mix one tablespoon glazing medium, one tablespoon burnt sienna, and one tablespoon burnt umber to make a dark stain.
4. Brush dark stain on the shelves and all edges. Blot as necessary, but don't rub off any color. The sconces will look best if the shelves and edges are darker than the background. Let dry.

Finishing:
Apply two coats of satin varnish. Let dry and sand between coats. Varnish the undersides and backs as well, so the wood will not warp. ❏

95

Embroidered Basket Linen Hanger

The design for this piece came from the embroidered linen dresser scarf you see displayed on it. You could use the woodburning pattern to create a matching embroidered piece.

Here's How

Preparation:
1. Sand wood lightly with fine sandpaper, paying close attention to curves around the edge and lightly rounding off sharp edges.
2. Trace and transfer design.

Woodburning:
Outlining is the only woodburning technique used on this project.
1. Prepare and heat woodburner.
2. With the mini-flow point, outline all design elements.
3. Erase all pencil and transfer marks. Wipe away any dust.

Coloring:
1. Color the designs with the colored pencils, using these colors:
   Basket - imperial violet
   Flowers - Mulberry, touched with hot pink
   Flower centers - lemon yellow
   Ribbon - pink rose
   Leaves - green
   Blend all colors with white, and layer as needed for bright color.
2. Blow away, then wipe off any pencil debris

You'll Need

Wooden Piece:
Medium size linen hanger with dowel rod

Woodburning Tools:
Woodburner with mini-flow point
Workspace set-up supplies

Oil Color Pencils:
Green
Hot pink
Imperial violet
Lemon yellow
Mulberry
Pink rose
White

Finishes:
Matte acrylic sealer spray
Optional: Matte or satin varnish

Other Tools & Supplies:
3/4" flat white bristle paintbrush
General supplies as listed in "Supplies" chapter

that may have accumulated from the coloring. (If it remains on the raw wood, it will smear when varnish is applied.)

Finishing:
1. Spray the entire piece, back and front, with two coats of matte sealer. Allow to dry and sand between coats. (The first layer of spray varnish sets the pencil and prevents smearing.)
2. *Option:* Add one or two coats of matte or satin varnish after spraying. Be sure to varnish the dowel. ❑

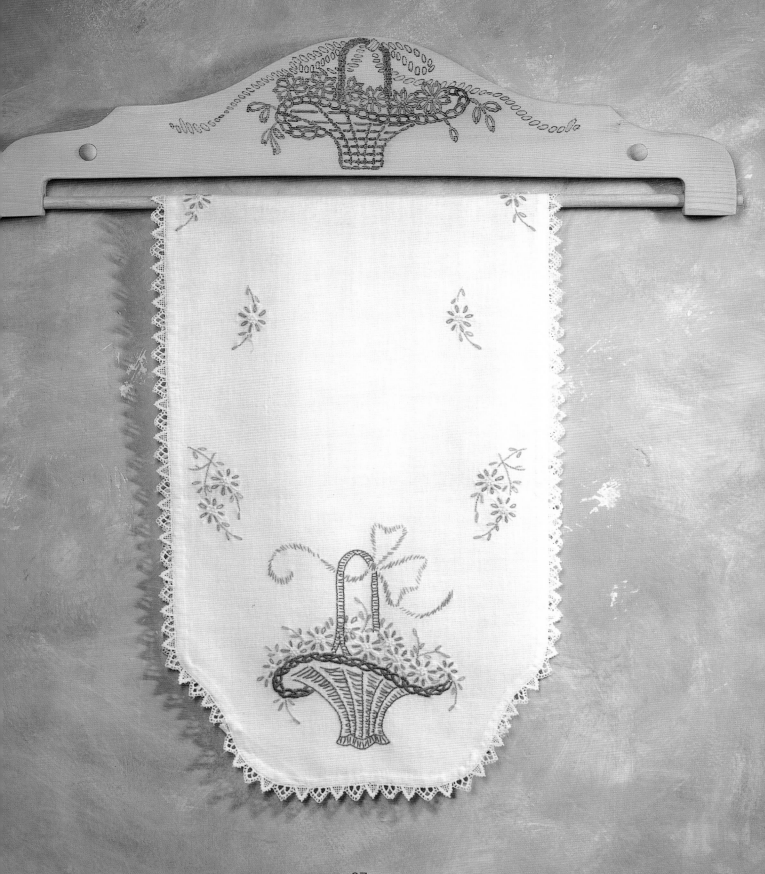

TWIN KITTIES CABINET

This is an easy project and recommended for beginners. The cat pattern is repeated on the second door, and the scarf design on the top can be any size.

HERE'S HOW

Preparation:
1. Remove the wooden knobs from the cabinet if you plan to replace them. A dull table knife is handy for loosening and prying off the knobs.
2. With fine sandpaper, sand with the grain, and lightly round off sharp edges.
3. Trace and transfer cat design to each door.
4. Trace and transfer the pattern for the scarf.

Woodburning:
The woodburning techniques used on this project are outlining, dots, fill-in, and wavy lines.
1. Prepare and heat woodburner.
2. With the flow point, outline all design elements on the kitties and the scarf.
3. Add dots on the neck ribbons and around the fringe on the top.
4. Indicate the fur with wavy lines.
5. Fill in the backs of the ears, inside the ribbons, and in the eyes and mouth. Fill in the shadows between the feet.
6. Erase all pencil and transfer marks. Wipe away any dust.

Coloring:
When mixed with glazing medium, paint colors are much lighter than they are in the bottle. Adjust the amount of paint or glaze as needed.
1. Mix the colors:
   - One tablespoon glazing medium and one tablespoon naphthol crimson.
   - One teaspoon glazing medium and one

YOU'LL NEED

Wooden Piece:
Small pine cabinet

Woodburning Tools:
Woodburner with flow point
Workspace set-up supplies

Acrylic Paints & Medium:
Neutral glazing medium
Acrylic Paints:
    Yellow light
    Naphthol crimson

Finish:
Gloss varnish

Other Tools & Supplies:
3/4" flat white bristle paintbrush
1/2" flat white sable paintbrush
Optional: 2 small brass knobs with screws and screwdriver
General supplies as listed in "Supplies" chapter

teaspoon yellow light.
2. Paint the eyes and neck ribbons with the yellow mix. Blot excess. Rub off some of the glaze with a rag.
3. Paint the kitties with the crimson mix. Blot. Rub off some of the glaze. Be careful not to paint or rub over the yellow sections.
4. Paint the scarf on the top of the cabinet with the crimson mix, using photo as a guide. Blot, then rub off the excess glaze. Let dry.

Finishing:
1. Apply at least two coats of satin varnish. Let dry and sand between coats. Be sure to varnish the inside of the doors and cabinet so the cabinet won't warp.
2. Attach the brass knobs to the doors. (If you keep the wooden knobs, be sure to give them plenty of varnish.) ❏

EQUINE WASTEBASKET

This wastebasket is a perfect gift for the horse lover. A number of designs from this book would work well on this wooden wastebasket.

HERE'S HOW

Preparation:

1. With fine sandpaper, sand lightly with the grain, paying close attention to curves around the edge and lightly rounding off sharp edges.
2. Trace and transfer horse design, centering on front of wastebasket.
3. Use ruler and pencil to draw a frame around the horses.
4. Trace and transfer ornate motif above the horses. Then turn wastebasket upside down and transfer the motif again. See photo for placement.
5. Pencil in a curving line 3/4" down from the top edge of the wastebasket on all four sides. (This is where the gold trim will be placed.)

Woodburning:

The woodburning techniques used on this project are outlining, dots, and fill-in.

1. Prepare and heat woodburner.
2. With the flow point, outline all design elements, including horses, trees, and trough.
3. Add details on the horses and fill in their eyes with the mini flow point, leaving some unburned area in each eye for a highlight.
4. Add details to the water.
5. Outline both ornate motifs with the flow point.
6. Burn a row of dots to form a frame around the horses.
7. Erase all pencil and transfer marks. Wipe away any dust.

Staining:

1. Paint the rectangle containing the horse design with two coats of satin varnish. Let dry and sand between coats. Be sure to cover the area all the way to the dots that surround the design. (This protects the area from stain during the next step.)
2. Mix two tablespoons light red oxide with an equal amount of burnt sienna. Add four tablespoons of glazing medium. Paint

YOU'LL NEED

Wooden Piece:
Medium birch wastebasket

Woodburning Tools:
Woodburner with flow point and mini-flow point
Workspace set-up supplies

Acrylic Paints & Medium:
Neutral glazing medium
Acrylic Paints:
    Burnt sienna
    Light red oxide
    Pure gold metallic

Oil Color Pencil:
Dark brown *or* burnt sienna

Finish:
Satin varnish

Other Tools & Supplies:
3/4" flat white bristle paintbrush
Small round paintbrush
General supplies as listed in "Supplies" chapter

the entire wastebasket, inside and out, except for the horses and the ornate motifs. Blot, then rub off some of the color to reveal the wood grain underneath.

Painting:

1. Using the small round paintbrush or a small flat paintbrush, paint the ornate motifs with pure gold, avoiding the woodburning. If you do get paint on the woodburning, wipe it off with a cotton swab. Touch up with a brown oil pencil after the paint has dried.
2. Paint the band around the top of the wastebasket with pure gold, including the very top edge. Let dry.

Finishing:

Apply two coats of satin varnish to the entire wastebasket, inside and out. Let dry and sand between coats. ❑

WOODBURNED JEWELRY

Woodburning also can be used to decorate wooden jewelry. Many small pre-cut wooden shapes are available to be fashioned into wonderful jewelry pieces. These designs are accented with wire and beads. Be careful when steadying these small wooden pieces because your hand will be very close to the point of the woodburner.

Angel on My Heart Pin

HERE'S HOW

Preparation:
1. Drill seven small holes around the point of the heart, spacing them 1/2" apart and placing them 1/4" from the edge of the wood.
2. Sand the pieces front and back, using fine grit sandpaper to smooth the wood around the drilled holes.
3. Since there are no patterns needed, you may not feel comfortable just free-burning the designs. If this is the case, use a pencil to draw in the lines for burning.

Woodburning:
The woodburning techniques used on this project are fill-in, wavy lines, and circles. No patterns are needed for this since this is simply a sampler of woodburning line techniques. You may use examples shown on pages 22 and 23 to fill in the design area.
1. Prepare and heat woodburner.
2. With the mini-flow point, burn the scallops on the wings, then the other details on the angel.
3. Burn the small circles over the entire surface of the heart.
4. Erase all pencil and transfer marks. Wipe away any dust.

Coloring:
1. Mix equal amounts glazing medium and Turner's yellow paint. Brush the mix on the front of the heart and wipe off. If more color is needed, add more paint and another coat of glaze, then wipe again. *Option:* Add a little burnt sienna to the glaze.
2. Color the angel's halo with the yellow pencil.

Finishing:
Apply two coats of gloss varnish to the angel, front and back. Let dry.

YOU'LL NEED
Wooden Pieces:
Narrow basswood heart
Large basswood angel cut-out

Woodburning Tools:
Woodburner with mini-flow point
Workspace set-up supplies

Acrylic Paints & Medium:
Neutral glazing medium
Acrylic Paints:
   Turner's yellow
   Optional: Burnt sienna

Oil Color Pencil:
Yellow *or* canary yellow

Finish: Gloss acrylic varnish

Other Tools & Supplies:
White glue or wood glue
24 gauge gold jewelry wire
20-24 small gold beads
10-15 small yellow and/or amber glass beads
1-1/2" pin back
Round nose pliers
Wire cutters
Small hand or electric drill
1/2" flat paintbrush
Small round paintbrush
General supplies as listed in "Supplies" chapter

Assembling the Pin:
1. Spread glue over the entire back of the angel and position it on the heart, using photo as a guide. Hold tightly with your fingers for a few seconds, then wipe away any glue that may have oozed out. Set a book or other heavy object on the pin.
2. With the wire cutters, cut a 10-12" length of gold wire. Use the round nose pliers to bend a tight curlicue in one end of the wire. String on two or three beads, then insert the other end of the wire from the front of the pin into the upper hole on one side. String on enough glass and gold beads to cover about 1" of wire, wind it up from behind, and insert the straight end in the next hole. Adjust the number of beads on the wire as needed, referring to the photo.

Continued on page 104

Angel on My Heart Pin (continued)

3. Continue "sewing" with the beaded wire, adjusting the beads as you go. When you reach the last hole on the first side of the heart, cut the wire to 1/2" and tightly curl the end, tucking under any sharp point so it won't snag your clothing.

4. Repeat the process with the holes on the other side of the heart.

5. Glue the pin back high on the back of the pin, pushing the pin back down into the glue until some of it oozes up through the holes. Hold for a few seconds, wipe off excess, and set aside to dry. ❑

Heart Photo Pin

See photo on page 103

HERE'S HOW

Preparation:

1. Drill six or seven small holes around the point of the heart, spacing them 1/2" apart and placing them 1/4" from the edge of the wood. Drill one hole at the top of the heart.
2. Sand the piece front and back, using fine grit sandpaper to smooth the wood around the drilled holes.
3. Since there are no patterns needed, you may not feel comfortable just free-burning the designs. If this is the case, use a pencil to draw in the lines for burning.

Woodburning:

The woodburning techniques used on this pin are fill-in, basket weave, coils, curving parallel lines, and a combination of parallel lines and dots. No pattern is needed. See pages 22 & 23 for examples of these woodburning lines.

1. Prepare and heat woodburner.
2. With the mini-flow point, burn the patterns on each section, letting them meet in the center. (The frame will be glued over the area where they meet, so you don't need to completely finish this part of the heart.)
3. Erase all pencil and transfer marks. Wipe away any dust.

Finishing:

Apply two coats of gloss or satin varnish on the heart, front and back. Let dry.

Adding the Charms & Photo:

1. Remove the brass backing from the charm frame. Trim the photo to size. Insert in the frame. Replace the back, bending the tabs to hold it in place.
2. Glue the framed photo to the front of the heart, using photo as a guide for placement. Press the frame into the glue and

YOU'LL NEED

Wooden Piece:
Narrow basswood heart

Woodburning Tools:
Woodburner with mini-flow point
Workspace set-up supplies

Finish:
Gloss or satin acrylic varnish

Other Tools & Supplies:
1/2" flat paintbrush
Small round paintbrush
White craft glue
Brass photo frame charm with back
Small photo for frame
Variety of small brass heart charms
Selection of large and small brass jump rings
1-1/2" pin back
Needlenose pliers
Wire cutters
Hand or electric drill
General supplies as listed in "Supplies" chapter

wipe away any excess that oozes out. Weight with a book until glue is set.

3. For the charms at the bottom, insert two or three small jump rings into the hanger on the top of each heart charm, creating a chain of jump rings so the heart will hang down. Attach each heart chain to a large jump ring. Attach the jump rings to the heart through the drilled holes.
4. For the charms at the top of the heart, make a shorter chain of jump rings. Cluster two or three small heart charms on it. Attach to top of heart with a large jump ring. ❑

PATTERNS FOR PROJECTS

This section includes patterns for the projects. They may not be actual size, but if not, a % of enlargement is given to bring them to actual size. They can be traced from the book then enlarged on a photocopier to fit your project surface.

Butterfly Tray

PAGE 34

Enlarge @143% for actual size.

Brace

Rustic Lilies Bench
PAGE 38
Enlarge @167% for actual size.

Top

106

Leafy Plant Table

PAGE 42

Actual Size Pattern

Border

Medallion

Repeat on
all corners

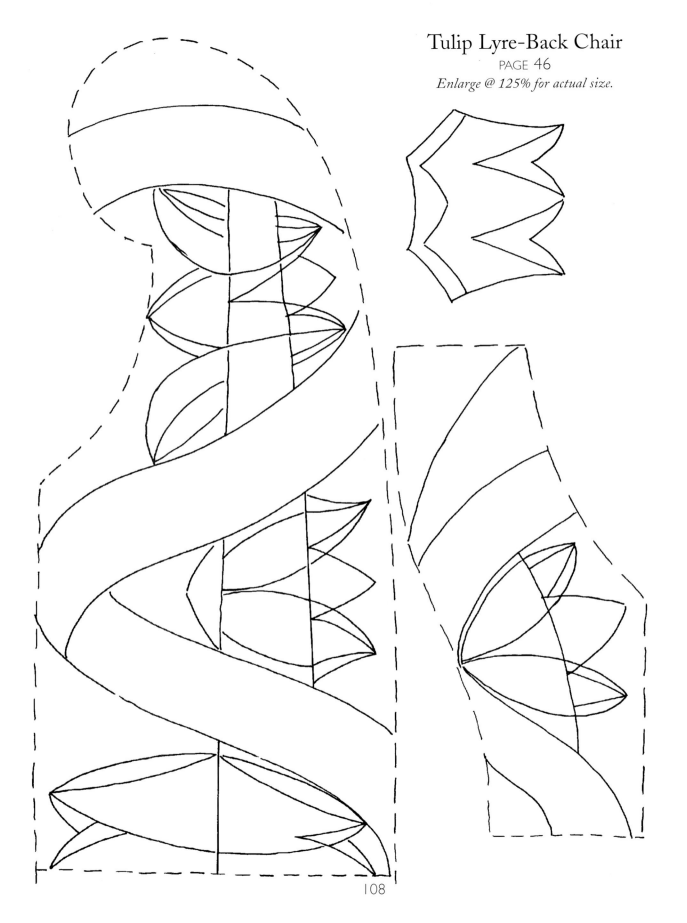

Tulip Lyre-Back Chair
PAGE 46
Enlarge @ 125% for actual size.

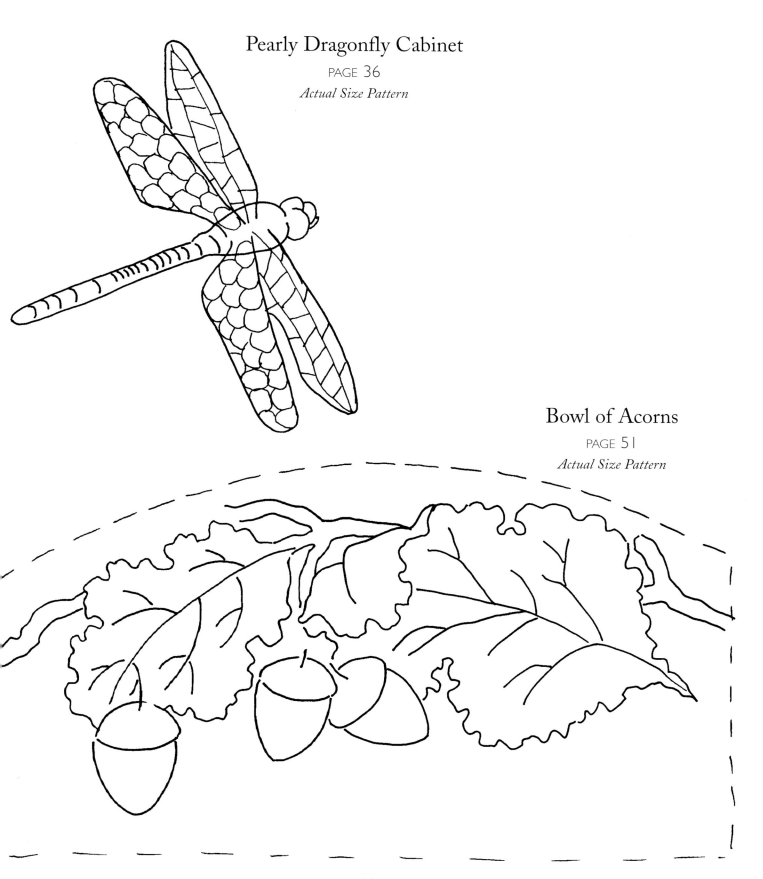

Pearly Dragonfly Cabinet

PAGE 36

Actual Size Pattern

Bowl of Acorns

PAGE 51

Actual Size Pattern

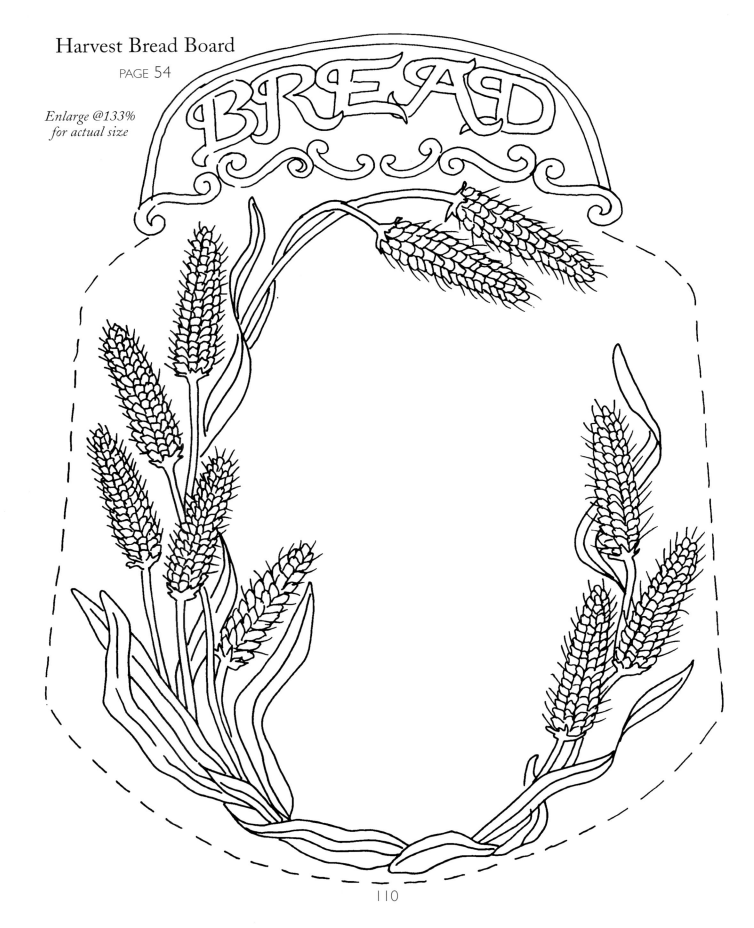

Harvest Bread Board

PAGE 54

*Enlarge @133%
for actual size*

BREAD

Actual Size Pattern

Use portion of vine for knife handles. Join dotted lines to complete pattern for knife block.

Vivid Candle Box
PAGE 64

Fantasy Flowers Tray
PAGE 61
Enlarge @ 143% for actual size.

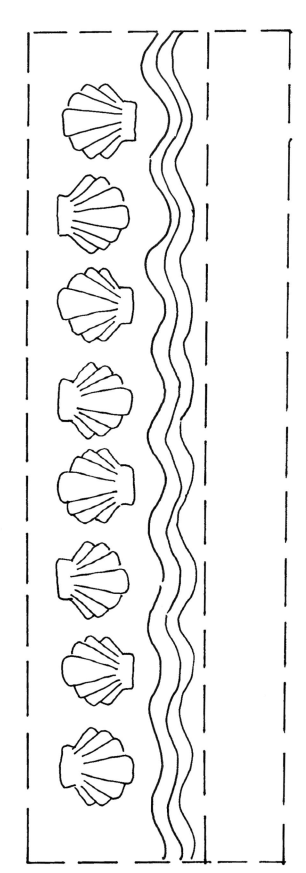

Base

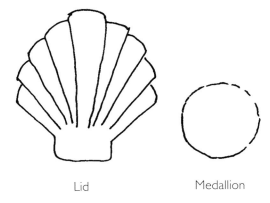

Lid　　　　Medallion

Elegant Photo Box

Box lid

Actual Size Patterns

Sides of lid

Two Fishes Box

PAGE 69

Actual Size Pattern

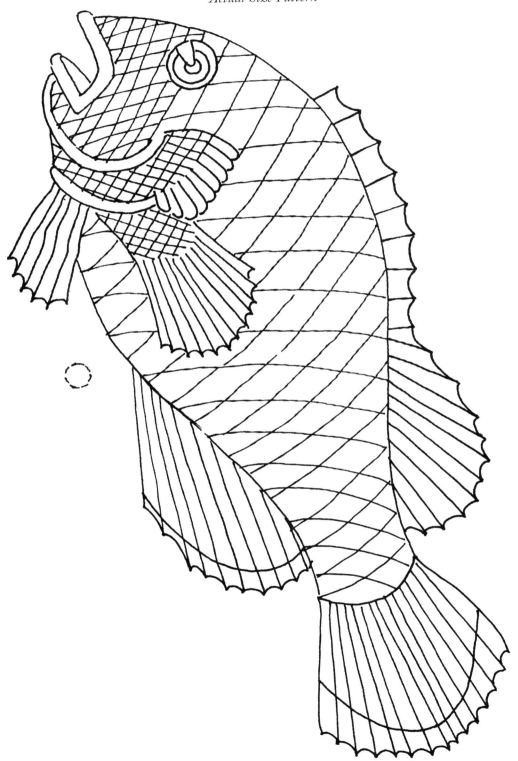

Leaves & Circles Photo Album

Actual Size Pattern

Spine

Cover

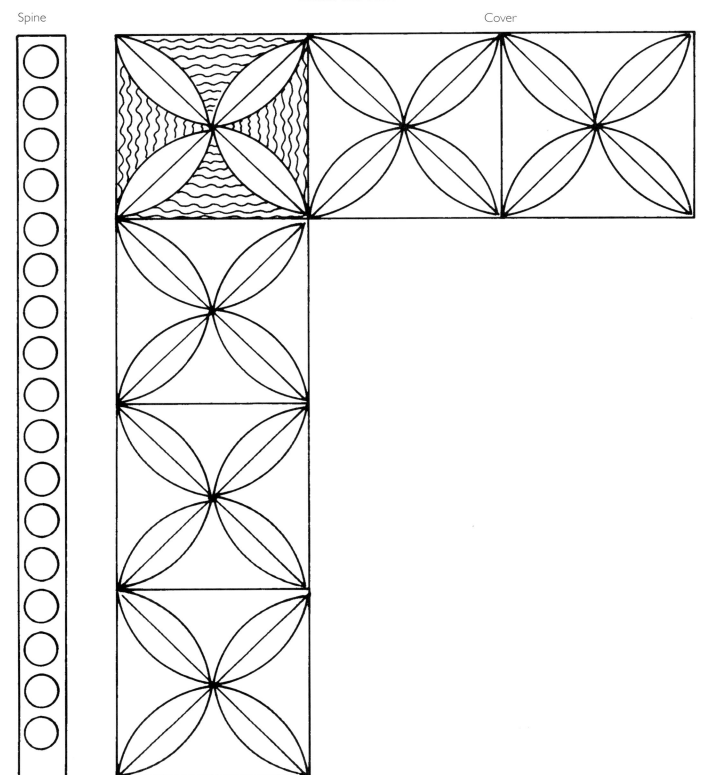

Victorian Sweetheart Frame

PAGE 78

Enlarge @ 133% for Actual Size

Flower Garland Corner Shelf

PAGE 81

Actual Size Pattern

Up

Dainty Tilting Clock

PAGE 90

Actual Size Patterns

Side

Face

Base

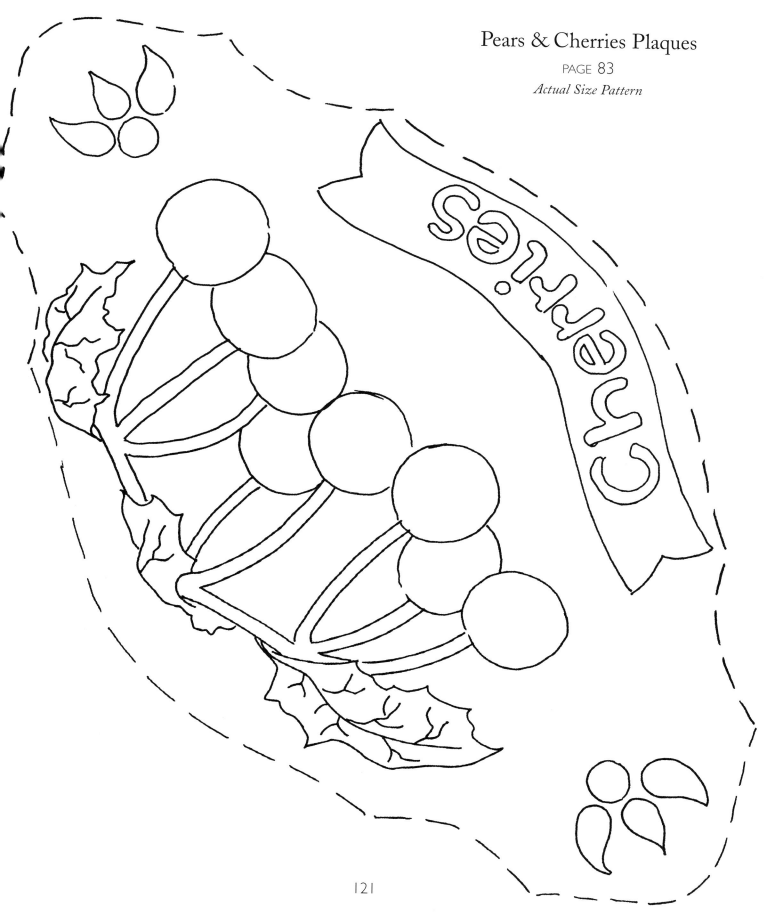

Pears & Cherries Plaques

PAGE 83

Actual Size Pattern

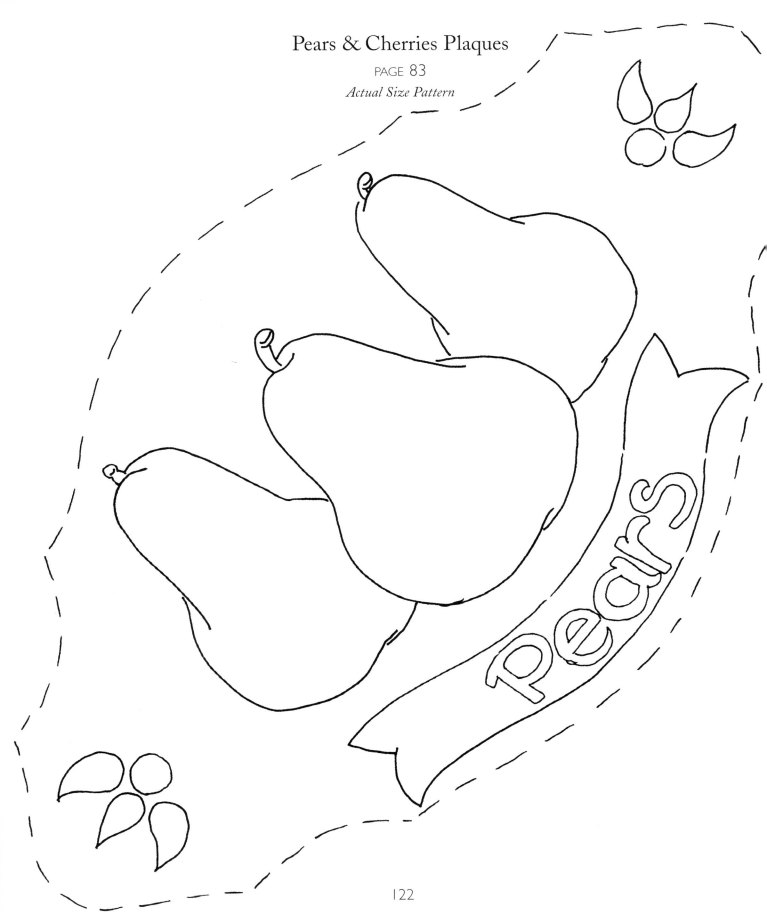

Pears & Cherries Plaques

PAGE 83

Actual Size Pattern

pears

Folk Art Star Boxes

PAGE 86

Enlarge all @ 133% for actual size.

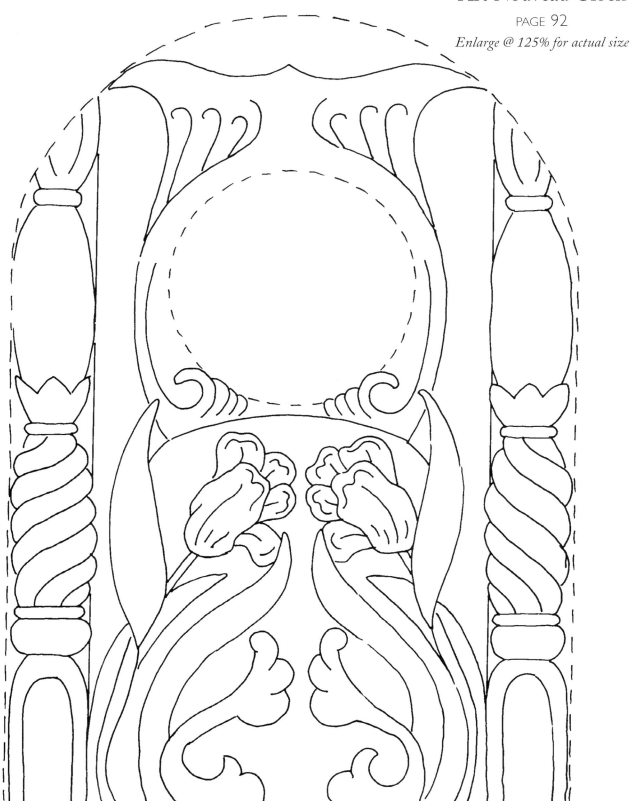

Candle Sconces

PAGE 94

Actual Size Patterns

Equine Wastebasket

PAGE 100

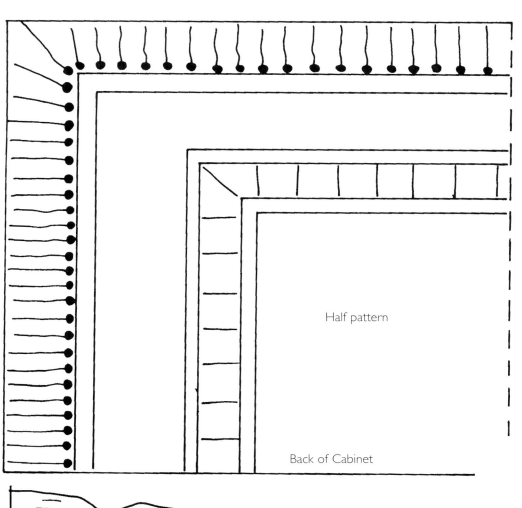

Half pattern

Back of Cabinet

Door Panel

Metric Conversion Chart

Inches to Millimeters and Centimeters

Inches	MM	CM
1/8	3	.3
1/4	6	.6
3/8	10	1.0
1/2	13	1.3
5/8	16	1.6
3/4	19	1.9
7/8	22	2.2
1	25	2.5
1-1/4	32	3.2
1-1/2	38	3.8
1-3/4	44	4.4
2	51	5.1
3	76	7.6
4	102	10.2
5	127	12.7
6	152	15.2
7	178	17.8
8	203	20.3
9	229	22.9
10	254	25.4
11	279	27.9
12	305	30.5

Yards	Meters
1/8	.11
1/4	.23
3/8	.34
1/2	.46
5/8	.57
3/4	.69
7/8	.80
1	.91
2	1.83
3	2.74
4	3.66
5	4.57
6	5.49
7	6.40
8	7.32
9	8.23
10	9.14

Embroidered Basket Linen Hanger

PAGE 96

Enlarge @ 143% for Actual Size

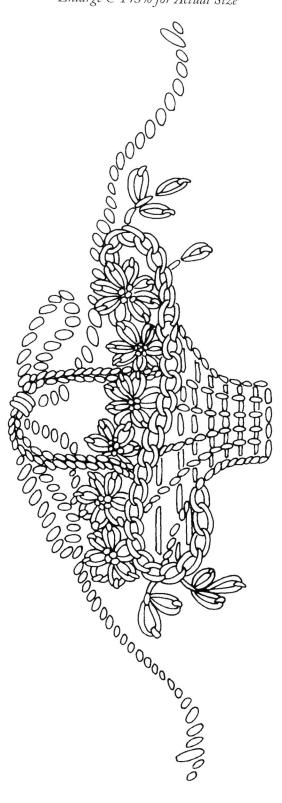

INDEX